THE
Nine Seasons
COOKBOOK

THE

Nine Seasons

COOKBOOK

More than 150 recipes to get you from
mud season to fall foliage and back again.

by Pat Haley

YANKEE BOOKS

A division of Yankee Publishing Incorporated
Dublin, New Hampshire

The Breast of Lamb with Fruited Rice Stuffing (page 56) was created by Georgia Doherty of the American Lamb Council.

The recipes on pages 51–53 from the New Hampshire Cooking Contest were provided by the National Broiler Council, sponsor of the National Chicken Cooking Contest.

Edited by Andrea Chesman
Designed by Margo Letourneau
Illustrated by Maryann Mattson

Yankee Publishing Incorporated
Dublin, New Hampshire 03444
First Edition
Second Printing, 1986
Copyright 1986 by Pat Haley

Library of Congress Catalog Card Number 85-51874
ISBN 0-89909-093-1

Dedication

For Francis and Eva

Contents

Preface

For me, cooking turned out to be one more country pleasure. When I lived in New York City, it was easier and more exciting to let chefs do the cooking. I dined out cheaply or luxuriously, depending on the state of my pocketbook or who invited me to dinner. Like many New Yorkers, I rarely went to the same restaurant twice. There were too many others waiting to be tried.

Eating at home meant eating take-out food. Then the dilemma was choosing between a Carnegie Deli hot pastrami sandwich or Chinese to go. Bakeries — two or three to a block — tempted me with cheesecake, chocolate torte, and fruit tarts. On the few occasions I cooked dinner, I shopped on the way home from work, buying just enough food for that meal. No one I knew had enough cupboard space to store a five-pound bag of flour.

In those days, I was a flight attendant, and sometimes I brought home lobsters from Boston or sourdough bread from San Francisco. On layovers, I often ate alone in sterile hotel restaurants where the only item I could afford, a hamburger, cost as much as a fine meal in more civilized places.

In some cities, good local food was served in downtown hotels. In New Orleans, for example, there was chicory coffee and croissants. In Omaha, the specialty was steak and eggs for breakfast.

Then I married a man who lived in an 1815 house at the edge of a New Hampshire forest. There were no other houses in sight.

Gradually, nature and the seasons began setting my daily agenda. Nature's calendar, a country dweller learns, is subtly drawn. Winter does not turn into spring on March 21. In fact, I have discovered at least nine seasons that evoke a response from people who live in this climate. City friends who ask what we do all winter don't know about cabin fever season, mud season, or sugaring season.

The land itself urged me toward the country arts: gardening, wine making, canning, and bread baking. At the same time, I started a new career writing for a daily newspaper.

Most nights of the week, I dined in. Good food is available in rural New England if you are willing to drive the distance to a country inn. But sometimes the weather makes the drive over an icy mountain a fool's journey. Other times, it is impossible to arrive before the inn's dining room closes for the night at eight thirty.

I invited my hungry, single exurbanite colleagues home to dinner. They brought lobsters, leeks, wine, and spices and recipes from their travels to India and Africa. The sampler that hangs in my kitchen came true. It reads, Good Cooks Never Lack Friends. It isn't so much that I am a good cook; rather, I enjoy breaking bread with those I care about.

My husband, Edward, was the one who suggested I write a cooking column. "You get so excited about working with food," he said. The first columns were timid, tentative. What would happen to my readers if I ran out of ideas? That never happened. Instead, my future file bulges with topics I plan to explore someday.

Then some of my tidier readers asked me to publish a collection of the columns, because they wanted all their favorite recipes in one place. However, many of the columns did not pass the test of time. Some endured, and I am grateful to publisher James D. Ewing and editor James A. Rousmaniere, Jr., for permission to print material that appeared in *The Keene Sentinel*.

I hope you will enjoy this taste of the country.

Chapter One

Wintered In

A n ancient tradition holds that what you do on the first day of the year sets the mood for the next 364. That's why New Year's Day is a fine time to organize a cross-country ski outing. It seems so appropriate to enter a fresh year enjoying the sparkling winter air with good friends. Friends become especially treasured during this long, dark season.

You see, January's unrelenting cold, ice, and snow set off cabin fever attacks among the most stable citizens. Up here, we relieve this stir craziness by gathering together and dancing the demons of darkness away. And by eating fiery snacks invented by Thais who have too much sense to live in this tundra.

We invite friends to share a pot of soul-warming soup. As the broth simmers, it releases moisture into the air, now bone-dry from the wood stove. Over the soup, we commiserate about frozen pipes and car batteries that won't start. Yet, by the end of January, one of us will say, "Yes, but did you notice it's still light at five o'clock now?"

Hot Drinks for
Cold Cross-Country Skiers

Whereas Christmas Eve draws the biggest crowds of nonchurchgoers to services, New Year's Day sends the sedentary to the slopes. Cross-country skis and snowshoes whoosh and crunch over the trails and meadows.

Every New Year's athlete seems to sport shiny new gear. Down parka cocoons and ski masks offer no clues to the identity of people puffing by. It is difficult to tell the Bostonian who's up here for a breath of fresh air from the villager who's breaking in a new pair of snowshoes or knickers.

I suspect there is something deep in our psyche ordering us out of the armchair and into the cold on the first day of the year. Perhaps if we go public with our resolutions on the first day of the year, the gods will reward us with a burning desire to burn calories all year long. This self-deception is probably related to the annual January blitz of magazine articles about quick-and-easy, no-fail diets.

However, people who spend New Year's Day on the slopes earn their refreshment. For a quick defrosting of the heart and hand, I recommend a steaming brew.

The word "mulled" comes to mind. To mull means to heat cider or wine with spices. The origins of the word are somewhat muddled. The *Oxford English Dictionary* says the word comes from the Middle English "to pulverize." Or, continues the *OED*, mull may originate in the Dutch word for becoming mad — something you might do if you drink too much. I came across the noun "muller" in a catalog of early American tools. The illustration showed a tool resembling a fireplace poker, and I envisioned our ancestors plunging a red-hot muller into a tankard of cider to warm it on a cold night.

I like the names of two traditional New England drinks more than the potions themselves. They are flips and a "yard of flannel." Flips are hot drinks warmed by thrusting an iron flip, or loggerhead, into a mug of ale, resulting in a pleasant sizzle and a burned taste. A "yard of flannel" consists of hot ale combined with beaten eggs, sugar, nutmeg, and rum. The ale and the egg mixture are poured back and forth between two pitchers until the mixture is creamy and as smooth as the fabric for which it is named.

When you invite friends to sit by the fire and sip warm cider you are repeating part of the wassailing or "apple-howling" ceremony of Devonshire, England. The rite is rooted in the festival honoring Pomona, the goddess of fruit trees. The wassailing was performed January 6. After the farmer, family, and guests ate their share of cakes and cider, a cake soaked in cider was placed in the branches of the finest apple tree in the orchard. Cider was sprinkled near the roots of the trees and the revelers danced a ring-around-the-apple-tree, inviting the goddess to bless the coming year's crop.

Modern recipes for mulled drinks call for whole spices, such as cinnamon, allspice, and cloves, plus spirals of lemon, orange, and tangerine rind.

The Swedish glogg is one pleasant mulled wine. The traditional version calls for placing a one-pound lump of sugar on a rack over a pot holding a gallon of dry red wine. The sugar is drenched with brandy and set aflame. It melts and drips into the heated wine. I prefer a less spectacular but safer version of glogg because I live out in the country, and on a freezing night our volunteer fire department prefers to douse a chimney fire rather than an out-of-control flambeau.

You can heat apple cider with spices for children and adults who don't want a spirited drink. One thoughtful hostess provides a tureen of steaming bouillon for guests who are dieting or on their way to work the night shift.

But for the others, a hot buttered rum or a warm wine punch is welcome. The word punch comes from the Hindu word *panch,* meaning five. The Indian punch had five ingredients: tea, water, sugar, lemon, and *arak,* an oriental spirit with a flavor recalling licorice.

You can flavor coffee or chocolate drinks with a shake of cinnamon, nutmeg, or cloves. For a spirited beverage, add amaretto, orange, or mint liqueur to either drink. And, of course, coffee and chocolate complement each other.

Tea and lemon, lime, or orange juice blend nicely for a hot drink. Or try tea with apple, cranberry, or pineapple juice.

Hot drinks are best served in mugs because they warm the hands that hold them. A small mug is the wisest way to serve alcoholic hot drinks. The Gaels called their little mugs noggins.

The following are some favorite defrosters.

The toast is from Alfred Lord Tennyson.

> Ring out the old, ring in the new,
> Ring, happy bells, across the snow;
> The year is going, let him go;
> Ring out the false, ring in the true.

Mulled Cider
Yield: 8 (6-ounce) servings

1 quart apple cider
2 cups orange juice
8 whole cloves
8 whole allspice
  berries
2 cinnamon sticks (4
  inches each)
8 ounces brandy
  (optional)

Mix all the ingredients, except the brandy, in a large kettle. Bring to a boil, reduce the heat to low, and simmer for 10 minutes. Keep warm over low heat.

If you desire a spirited drink, add 1 ounce brandy to each serving.

Glogg Simplified

Yield: 8 (4-ounce) servings

1 quart dry red wine,
  such as Burgundy
¼ cup sugar
¼ cup raisins
¼ cup slivered
  almonds
4-inch cinnamon
  stick, broken into a
  few pieces
8 whole cloves
4 whole allspice
  berries
¼ teaspoon ground
  nutmeg

Combine all the ingredients in a large pot. Stir and bring almost to a boil, but do not boil. Keep warm on very low heat. I use my crockery pot on the low setting.

For larger groups, I use a 30-cup coffee urn for serving the brew.

This glogg recipe can be multiplied as many times as needed. The leftover glogg can be stored in the refrigerator and reheated.

For a thoughtful gift, you can mix the dry ingredients, place them in a small plastic bag, and put them into a basket with a bottle of wine and the recipe.

German Glee Wine

Yield: 16 (4-ounce) servings

2 lemons
1 quart dry red wine,
  such as Burgundy
  or claret
2 cups water
12 whole cloves
6 whole allspice
  berries
4-inch cinnamon stick
¼ teaspoon ground
  ginger
2 cups orange juice
¼ to ½ cup sugar

Gluhwein is German for mulled wine. It is a specialty at ski lodges run by German-American families. Somehow, in the spirit of things, this recipe came to be called glee wine.

* * *

Using a vegetable parer, remove the rind from the lemons. Squeeze the lemons and strain the juice.

Place the rinds, lemon juice, and all other ingredients in a large pot and bring almost to a boil. Do not boil. Keep warm over low heat.

John Fife's Grog

Yield: 1 serving

1 cup apple cider
1½ ounces light rum
1 tablespoon pure
    maple syrup
Juice of ½ lemon
3 whole cloves
1 slice lemon, for
    garnish
Cinnamon stick, for
    garnish

John Fife of Jaffrey, New Hampshire, banked on the fact that after people climb a mountain, they will pay anything for a warming or cooling drink. Fife opened a tavern on the summit of Mount Monadnock in 1824. That is the last time he is mentioned in local histories. I'll never know whether he prospered or not; but each time I climb Monadnock, I think about him. I named this cider drink after the mountaintop host.

* * *

For each serving, use the amounts listed above.

Heat the cider to boiling. Meanwhile, rinse a mug with hot water to preheat it.

Pour the cider into the mug. Stir in the rum, maple syrup, lemon juice, and cloves. Garnish with a slice of lemon and a stick of cinnamon. Serve at once.

Café Grand Marnier

Yield: 4 servings

½ cup heavy cream
2 tablespoons
    confectioners' sugar
1 teaspoon grated
    orange rind
3 cups fresh hot
    coffee
½ cup Grand Marnier
    or other orange-
    flavored liqueur
1 orange slice, cut into
    quarters

In a small bowl, beat the cream until stiff. Gently fold in the sugar and orange rind. Pour hot coffee into 4 mugs. Stir 2 tablespoons liqueur into each one. Top with the whipped cream mixture. Garnish with an orange wedge and serve at once.

Hot Spiced Tea

Yield: 16 (6-ounce) servings

3 quarts water
1-inch cinnamon stick
1 teaspoon whole
cloves
¼ teaspoon ground
nutmeg
Rind of 1 lemon, cut
into 2-inch chunks
Rind of 1 orange, cut
into 2-inch chunks
3 tablespoons black
tea leaves
½ to 1 cup sugar or ⅓
to ¾ cup honey

Bring the water, spices, and fruit rinds to a boil. Add the tea leaves and steep for 5 minutes. Tea starts to become bitter if it is allowed to steep for more than 5 minutes.

Strain the tea. Add the sugar or honey to taste. Keep warm over low heat.

Sally LaMar's Wassail Bowl

Yield: 40 (4-ounce) servings

1 gallon apple cider
1 unpeeled orange,
pierced with 12
whole cloves
1 can (6 ounces)
frozen orange juice
concentrate
¾ cup water
¼ cup firmly packed
brown sugar
6 whole cloves
½ teaspoon whole
allspice berries
2 cinnamon sticks (4
inches each)
1½ cups cognac or
brandy
½ cup pecan halves
1½ cups golden
raisins

Combine the cider, orange, orange juice concentrate, water, brown sugar, and spices in a large pot. Bring just to a boil and simmer for 10 minutes. Add the cognac or brandy, pecans, and raisins and serve at once in mugs. Or keep warm over low heat.

Cabin Fever Party:
Bring Your Favorite Snack
And Dancing Shoes

My friend Medora Hebert collects interesting people all year long. She is a photographer, and as she clicks her shutter at the face and faces of New England, she assembles a guest list for a big party.

Then when we need each other the most — in the cabin fever season — she sends out eighty invitations. Cabin fever is epidemic in the north country by mid-February. After eight weeks of winter, our once cozy houses begin to close in on us, and the gray, cold days chill the blood and the spirit.

When Medora's invitations arrive, we are ready to howl together to keep the grayness at bay. She pushes the furniture up against the walls and clears at least one room for dancing. She buys beer by the keg and wines by the jug and asks each guest to bring a favorite snack.

The guests are as diverse as the snacks. I have met tree surgeons, eye surgeons, detectives, reality therapists, carpenters, soccer coaches, and sci-fi writers. And I have tasted guacamole, *spanakopita,* crab dip, *baba ghanouj,* curried almonds, spicy ribs, maple fudge, mint chocolate chip cookies, and tiny Reuben sandwiches.

Of course, sampling food is a lot like sampling people. There are surprises in each: You can soar with the taste of ripe Brie or the racy wit of an art historian, or you can be stuck with a bowl of soggy chips or a bourbon-sogged boor.

Taste in both people and food is in the psyche of the beholder, and undoubtedly, I have served a soggy dish or idea now and then. For one cabin fever party, I baked a chocolate-toffee bar cookie that had to be smashed with a meat mallet before it could be chiseled from the pan. The directions said to bake it until done, but never revealed how long that might be, nor provided any clues about what doneness looked like. But it was too late to start all over. However, when I retrieved my plate at the party's end, the cookies were all gone.

Another time, I went for the grand statement and made a caviar mold served on a footed plate. I also prepared a Liptauer cheese served in a pumpernickel bowl. One time, I delegated the entire matter to the helpful owner of a cheese shop who sent me on my way for less than five dollars.

Toting a dish to a party is akin to the Yankee church supper, where many hands make light work and a bit of money for the church coffers. The good ladies of the Monadnock region churches bring substantial fare like baked beans, coleslaw, and apple pies.

But it takes a certain skill to carry a dish of food in midwinter when the paths between the car and house resemble the north face of the Matterhorn. Thus, many New Hampshire partygoers wear their chain-tread L. L. Bean boots to the party and carry their strappy dancing shoes. It is difficult to make a memorable entrance carrying a crockery pot, dancing shoes, and handbag and at the same time greet your hostess, who is somewhere beyond your fogbound eyeglasses.

Guests who are more soigné than I am carry long loaves of perfect bread swaddled in a red-and-white-checked napkin. Or baskets of cookies wrapped in clear plastic punctuated with a gold ribbon. One friend has solved the problem by tracking down an old-fashioned pie basket. The basket is made of wide strips of New Hampshire ash. It has handles for carrying and is deep enough to hold a casserole.

Just the sight of Katherine Pinkham Cox smiling over the top of her pie basket tells me we are all going to have a fine time at Medora's cabin fever party.

Here are some cabin fever favorites. Somehow, the recipe for the toffee bars escaped my filing system.

Celebration Caviar Mold   *Yield: 25 appetizer servings*

1 cup sour cream
1 cup cottage cheese
1 teaspoon lemon
   juice
½ teaspoon
   Worcestershire
   sauce
1 tablespoon minced
   onion
¼ cup dry sherry
1 envelope (1
   tablespoon)
   unflavored gelatin
4 ounces red or black
   caviar
Rye bread or crackers

In a food processor or blender, combine the sour cream, cottage-cheese, lemon juice, Worcestershire sauce, and onion. Process only until the mixture is smooth — about 10 seconds.

Place the sherry in a small saucepan. Sprinkle the gelatin over the sherry and let it stand for 3 to 4 minutes to soften. Then stir the mixture over low heat until dissolved. Combine the gelatin mixture and sour cream-cottage cheese mixture in a blender or food processor and mix briefly.

Pour into a lightly greased 2-cup mold. Refrigerate until firm. This will take at least 4 hours.

To unmold, loosen the sides with a knife and invert the mold onto a plate. Top with the caviar. Serve with rye bread or crackers.

Diane Wood's Hot Artichoke Dip

Yield: 3 cups

1 can (14 ounces)
   artichoke hearts,
   drained and
   chopped
1 can (4 ounces)
   chopped green
   chilies
1 cup Parmesan
   cheese
1 cup mayonnaise
½ teaspoon garlic
   powder
Dried or chopped
   fresh parsley
Tortilla chips

Mix together the artichokes, chilies, cheese, mayonnaise, and garlic powder. Place in a small casserole. Sprinkle with parsley.

Bake at 350°F. for 20 minutes. Serve warm with tortilla chips.

Hummus

Yield: 2 cups

1 can (20 ounces)
   chickpeas
¼ cup fresh lemon
   juice
2 garlic cloves,
   minced
2 tablespoons olive oil
4 tablespoons tahini
   or sesame seeds
Salt
Freshly ground
   pepper
Chopped fresh
   parsley
Paprika
Pita bread, warmed
   and cut into 2-inch
   triangles, or crisp
   raw vegetable
   sticks

Whenever I make this chickpea dip, I think of Connie Daniels, one of my New Hampshire readers. Every so often, Mrs. Daniels hailed me in the supermarket and asked me to list the dip's ingredients. "It's so easy, Connie," I protested. "Just make it once and you'll never forget it." I don't know whether she ever made the dip, but during the years we shopped at the same super-market, she enjoyed getting the recipe in the an-cient oral tradition.

* * *

Drain the chickpeas and reserve the liquid. In a blender or food processor, combine the chick-peas, lemon juice, garlic, 1 tablespoon of the olive oil, and the tahini or sesame seeds. Blend until smooth. Add enough reserved liquid to make a creamy consistency. Taste and add salt and pepper. Pile in a serving bowl and garnish with the remaining 1 tablespoon olive oil, pars-ley, and paprika. Store in the refrigerator until you are ready to serve. Serve with the pita bread triangles or vegetables.

Thai Chicken Wings

Yield: 5 to 6 servings as an appetizer
or 1 course in a Thai meal

2 pounds chicken
  wings
2 tablespoons peanut
  oil
⅓ cup dark soy sauce
2 tablespoons sherry
2 tablespoons honey
1 garlic clove, crushed
1 teaspoon finely
  grated fresh ginger
  root
Crushed hot red
  pepper

Susan Norlander grew up in Thailand. She is an artist who now farms with her husband and daughters in rural New Hampshire. People who know that Susan is coming to a potluck supper joyfully anticipate an artistic salad or a Thai specialty. Susan says the following recipe can be used with other chicken parts, "but somehow wings are more fun to eat!"

* * *

Remove the tips from the chicken wings and save them for making stock. Cut the remainder of each wing into 2 pieces. Heat the oil in a wok and fry the wing joints on high heat until browned, about 3 minutes. If your wok is not large enough to hold the wings in a single layer, brown the wings in batches.

Stir together the remaining ingredients, adding the hot pepper to taste, and add to the wok; stir well. Reduce the heat to low, cover the wok, and simmer until the wings are tender, about 30 minutes. Stir frequently after 15 minutes; the sweet glaze gets thick and might burn. Serve warm.

Crockery Pots:
A Clue to the State of Society

A row of crockery pots at a church supper or a PTA potluck dinner reveals more about the state of society than some doctoral theses on the topic.

The column of crockery pots marching across the buffet table is one more sign of our shifting American lifestyle. Many women have hung up their aprons to work outside the home for pay. But they not only bring home the bacon, they still have to cook it. Few cooks of either gender have time to do much more than mix ingredients. And if a pot needs watching, there is no one at home to do it.

Enter the crockery pot, or slow cooker. It needs neither watching nor stirring because of its low cooking temperature.

When family members have different schedules for an evening, each can dip into the pot when ready to eat.

The popularity of slow cookers also reflects the increased use of cheaper cuts of meat. People who once broiled steaks now cook stews. If it makes you feel less deprived, call your thrifty stew a pot-au-feu, a French term for a pot cooked over low heat on the back of a wood stove.

I used to make red wine beef stew in my oven because the low, even temperature allowed me to forget about the stew while I did other chores. But using a full-size oven to make stew these days is out of the question. I make my stew in a crockery pot, which consumes less energy. Crockery pots use slightly less fuel than cooking on top of the stove.

Before buying a slow cooker, consider borrowing one from a friend or relative. You might discover slow cooking is not for you. Some people don't want to surrender counter or cupboard space to one more small appliance. Others say every dish done in a crockery pot tastes the same, which is probably true if each recipe used calls for a can of cream of mushroom soup. And there are cooks who don't want to think about any meal until the last possible moment.

When selecting a slow cooker, it is a good idea to buy one with a separate pot. It may cost a few dollars more, but the convenience is worth the price. If the pot and the element are housed in a single unit, you cannot immerse the pot in water for scrubbing or soaking.

I like to use my cooker on weekends to prepare baked beans, tomato sauces, and soups and stews for the week ahead. If I happen to be using most of the kitchen, including the top of the stove for a full-scale production, I place the pot in another room, freeing both counter space and an electrical outlet.

During the holidays, you can use the pot to keep mulled wine or cider warm. In the summer, you can boil chicken for salad without adding more heat and humidity to the air. A slow cooker can be used for steaming breads and puddings.

At harvest, think about using a slow cooker without its cover for boiling down fruit butters, jams, catsup, and other easily scorched preserves. During the tomato harvest, I often have pizza sauce cooking down while I go about other chores. I freeze the finished sauce in pint containers.

One working mother I know introduced her three sons to cooking by starting them off at about the age of ten with slow cooker duty when they arrived home from school. Two of the boys never got much further than sloppy joes and easy Hawaiian chicken, but the third became a fine cook.

Most slow cookers have a high and a low setting. Whatever duty you assign to your crockery pot, remember the low setting cooks at approximately 200°F. and the high at about 300°. Thus, you can adapt many recipes accordingly.

It turns out there is an entire cookbook literature on slow cookers. One book suggests heating hot dogs in bottled barbecue sauce for 14 hours. The formula for "old-fashioned baked beans" in another cookbook calls for three cans of baked beans in tomato sauce, catsup, barbecue sauce, and brown sugar. For dessert, there are heated canned peaches with more brown sugar. But at least one cookbook offers all the standard recipes for soups and stews and converts them for the person who does a lot of crockery cooking.

And if someone does send you a carton of steaks from Omaha or lobsters from Maine, just remember you will be much better off cooking those treasures on top of the stove — very quickly.

The following hearty dishes can bubble away unattended most of the day. When diners enter the house from the cold, a welcoming aroma will forecast good things to come.

Beef Burgundy

Yield: 4 to 6 servings

2 pounds boneless beef chuck, cut into 1-inch pieces
⅓ cup flour
⅓ cup olive oil
2 beef bouillon cubes
2 cups hot water
2 garlic cloves, minced
1 can (6 ounces) tomato paste
1¼ cups Burgundy
½ pound small white onions
4 carrots, finely chopped
1 bay leaf
1 teaspoon dried thyme
2 teaspoons sugar
¼ cup unsalted butter
½ pound mushrooms, sliced
Egg noodles or rice (optional)

Organizing a potluck dinner is one way to enjoy good friends. I ask guests to bring a salad, bread, or dessert. I supply a no-fuss entrée, such as Beef Burgundy. If I have time, I like to buy a variety of red and white wines for tasting and comparing.

* * *

Coat the beef with the flour. In a large pot, heat the olive oil. Add the meat and brown quickly over high heat. Transfer the meat to a slow cooker.

Dissolve the bouillon cubes in the hot water. Add to the pot with the garlic, tomato paste, Burgundy, onions, carrots, herbs, and sugar. Stir gently.

Cover and cook on low for 5 to 7 hours. Just before serving, melt the butter in a pan and sauté the mushrooms until golden. Add them to the beef.

Serve over egg noodles or rice, if desired. Beef Burgundy can be made the day before serving and reheated.

Marion Faulkner's Pepper Pot
Yield: 6 to 8 servings

1 quart veal or
  chicken stock or
  water
1 veal knuckle and
  other gelatinous
  veal bones
1 cup chopped onion
1 cup chopped green
  pepper
½ pound tripe, cut
  small
1 tablespoon butter,
  melted
2 tablespoons
  uncooked rice
3 cups fresh or canned
  tomatoes
1 teaspoon sugar
Salt

Marion Faulkner's Pepper Pot was a Christmas tradition. "It's nice to have the soup simmering on the stove when the kids are to arrive Christmas Day but you don't know exactly when. Tripe may be unusual for some, but it is essential to the flavor," she explained. Here is her original recipe; it also works well with a slow cooker.

* * *

Combine the stock or water, bones, onion, green pepper, tripe, butter, and rice in a large saucepan and bring to a boil. Lower the heat and simmer for 2 hours. Add the tomatoes and sugar and cook for 20 minutes more. Pick off any meat on the bones and return to the soup. Add salt to taste. Serve.

Slow Cooker Method: Combine all the ingredients in a slow cooker. Cover and cook on low for 6 to 8 hours. Pick off any meat from the bones and return to the soup.

Minestrone
Yield: 6 servings

1 tablespoon olive oil
1 cup chopped onion
1 cup peeled and
  diced potato
½ cup chopped celery
1 teaspoon dried
  oregano
1 teaspoon dried basil
6 cups beef stock
1 can (16 ounces)
  tomatoes, with
  liquid
1 can (20 ounces)
  cannellini (white
  kidney beans)
½ cup dry red wine
1 cup raw macaroni
  (elbow or ditali)
Parmesan cheese

The name of this soup is rooted in the Latin word, minestrare, *to serve. Tradition holds that in the days before inns, travelers in Italy stopped at monasteries, where they were assured a bowl of hearty vegetable soup and a night's lodging. The ingredients in the soup varied from region to region.*

* * *

Combine all ingredients, except the macaroni and cheese, in a slow cooker. Cover and cook on low for 6 to 7 hours. Turn the heat to high, add the macaroni, and cook for 30 minutes, or until the macaroni is just tender. Sprinkle with Parmesan cheese just before serving.

Note: You can substitute red kidney beans or chickpeas for the cannellini.

Peter's Best Pot Roast

Yield: 6 servings

4-pound beef round or
  chuck pot roast
2 tablespoons flour
2 tablespoons
  vegetable oil
1 cup tomatoes
1 cup beef broth
2 garlic cloves,
  minced
1 grind fresh black
  pepper
1 cup chopped onion
¼ cup white distilled
  vinegar
¼ cup lemon juice
¼ cup catsup
2 tablespoons brown
  sugar
1 tablespoon
  Worcestershire
  sauce
1 teaspoon dry
  mustard
Cooked noodles, rice,
  or mashed potatoes

When my stepson, Peter Sullivan, was about 6 years old, he spent his summers in the country with my husband and me. I was the chief source of entertainment. When I cooked, Peter grilled me with questions, such as, "Why do you use sage?" or "What's a roux?" I replied in my best home economics teacher manner, and he became a great cook at the age of 13 or 14. This pot roast was one of his specialties. These days, Peter doesn't have time to cook because he has a full-time job and goes to law school. But when he finishes his studies, I expect we will once again enjoy that special kind of choreography only performed by 2 people cooking a meal for those they love.

* * *

Dredge the meat in the flour. In a large pot, heat the oil. Add the meat and brown quickly on all sides. Place the meat and the remaining ingredients in a slow cooker. Stir gently. Cover and cook on low for 8 to 10 hours. Serve with noodles, rice, or mashed potatoes to absorb all the great-tasting gravy.

The Garlic Cure
Can't Do Any Harm

"At the first sign of a cold, take a clove of garlic, remove the papery covering, split the clove in two, and place one half in each cheek. Let your whole system absorb the powerful garlic juice and get fast, fast relief from the symptoms of your cold."

If folk remedies ever make it to prime-time television, this is how the commercials might sound. But it's unlikely that anything as simple as the garlic cure will be mass-marketed.

Most cures — ingesting vitamin C in time-released capsules, baking in a sauna, sipping lemon toddies — are simply ways to avoid that sound medical prescription, bed rest. We would do anything to avoid taking the rest we need. It takes a certain degree of maturity to admit that the earth will continue rotating on its axis without our guidance. It takes maturity to suffer in solitude rather than share our snuffles and germs with everyone else.

Historically, the garlic cure is as controversial as today's vitamin C cure. In Egypt, according to one account, garlic was considered a powerful restorative but was also very rare. Only first-rank kings were buried with a bulb of the real thing at their sides. Ordinary people had to settle for clay replicas.

Another source says Egyptian priests declared garlic unclean and forbade its presence in the tombs of high-class humans. Workers were another matter. Greek historian Herodotus notes the Great Pyramid at Giza was built by workers whose strength was rooted in an onion-and-garlic diet.

Now comes word that scientific research could back up claims of garlic's healing powers. There is evidence that garlic may be useful in the treatment of such maladies as bacterial infection, diabetes, and heart disease, reports nutrition writer Dorothy Sly in *The Professional Nutritionist.*

In some parts of the world, the results of garlic research are already being applied in medicine. The bulb is the basis for acne and antibacterial creams used in Hungary and Yugoslavia. Russia imports tons of fresh garlic to help fight epidemics of flu. And in India, garlic therapy is reported to reduce blood cholesterol levels in humans.

"We don't know yet whether it can cure the common cold," Sly says, "but it is surely a low-sodium, low-fat way to enliven the diet."

Onions and garlic belong to the *Allium* genus as do shallots, leeks, and chives. A single bulb of garlic contains eight to twelve sections called cloves, which are held together by a papery skin.

When you buy garlic, remember that plumpness counts. Avoid the garlic sold in little cardboard boxes that prevent a close look at the bulb. More than one good cook has been misled into thinking those withered shards were garlic. If you shop where the produce is loose, you are more likely to find a fresh, firm bulb.

Store garlic in an open container at room temperature. I use a sugar bowl that lost its top.

Many recipes order you to peel garlic. Don't bother because it's a Sisyphean task. Instead, smash the clove with the side of a cleaver. The skin slips off and with a few more strokes, the garlic is minced.

Cooked garlic won't linger on your breath, but eaten in the raw, it will tell the world you had gazpacho for lunch and antipasto with dinner. Herbalists advise chasing the garlic with a few anise or caraway seeds. Chewing on fresh parsley also helps.

The Japanese have already worked out the problem of telltale breath and profited by it. A rice farmer switched to planting garlic when he observed a rising demand for the seasoning in the marketplace. When he succeeded in developing an odorless strain, his fortune was made.

It's difficult to imagine popping a chunk of garlic that would not take your breath away. Not to mention everyone you meet in the next hour.

Here is a hearty — if not healthy — selection of recipes calling for the odorous bulb.

Peg Newell's Garlic Vinegar
Yield: 1 quart

1 quart vinegar
12 garlic cloves

Peg Newell's Garlic Vinegar was a best seller in the pantry department of her church's Christmas bazaar. She made the vinegar in late May every year — and she never made a salad dressing without it.

* * *

Peg said to use any kind of vinegar you have on hand. Peel and split the garlic cloves in half. Place the vinegar and cloves in a glass jar and let it sit in a sunny window for 2 weeks. Strain the vinegar through a cloth or a funnel fitted with a coffee filter into a glass jar and store tightly capped.

Garlic Vinegar Salad Dressing
Yield: 1¼ cups

1½ teaspoons dry
  mustard
½ teaspoon salt
2 teaspoons flour
2 eggs
2 tablespoons sugar
2 tablespoons melted
  butter or vegetable
  oil
⅔ cup milk
¼ cup Garlic Vinegar
  (above)

Mix the mustard, salt, and flour in the top of a double boiler. Stir in the eggs, sugar, butter or vegetable oil, milk, and vinegar in the order given. This is important to prevent curdling. Cook the dressing over hot water until smooth. Cool to room temperature and sieve. Store extra dressing in the refrigerator.

Julia Older's Garlic Soup

Yield: 6 servings

3 tablespoons olive oil
1 cup cubed French
  bread (crouton size)
  left standing for 1
  to 2 hours
2 large garlic cloves
1 teaspoon paprika
⅛ teaspoon cayenne
  pepper
5 cups stock (half
  chicken, half beef)
2 eggs, slightly beaten
2 tablespoons minced
  fresh parsley
Salt

Julia Older is a poet and musician who lives in the Monadnock region of New Hampshire. Her books include Cooking Without Fuel *and* Soup & Bread *in collaboration with Steve Sherman.*

* * *

Heat the olive oil in a frying pan over medium-high heat. Add the croutons and brown in the oil. When the croutons are almost brown, press the garlic with the side of a knife, mince, and add to the pan.

Sauté the garlic and croutons approximately 3 minutes more. Remove three-quarters of the croutons and reserve.

Add the paprika, cayenne, and stock to the croutons remaining in the pan. Bring the soup to a fast boil. Remove the pan from the heat; then quickly stir in the eggs, parsley, and salt.

Cover and let stand for 5 minutes.

Warm individual soup bowls with hot water. Serve a few saturated croutons in each bowl, and let guests help themselves to the remaining crisp croutons at the table.

Spinach Quiche

Yield: 6 servings

Crust

1¼ cups unbleached
all-purpose flour
½ teaspoon salt
3 tablespoons
unsalted butter
3 tablespoons
shortening
1 egg yolk
3 to 4 tablespoons
cold water

Filling

4 tablespoons olive oil
1 garlic clove, minced
1 medium-size onion,
diced
1 cup chopped fresh
zucchini
½ cup chopped green
pepper
3 large eggs, slightly
beaten
1½ cups small-curd
cottage cheese
3 ounces cream
cheese, softened
and diced
½ teaspoon salt
⅛ teaspoon freshly
ground black
pepper
1 teaspoon dried dill
weed
½ teaspoon freshly
ground nutmeg
10 ounces spinach,
cooked, drained,
and chopped
⅓ cup grated
Parmesan cheese
½ cup cream

Steve Sherman is a writer who lives in Hancock, New Hampshire. His books include Cheese Sweets & Savories *and* Soup & Bread *in collaboration with Julia Older.*

This quiche is from Cheese Sweets & Savories. *Steve describes it as "rather thick, good for an entrée or, cut thinly, as an appetizer."*

* * *

Preheat the oven to 450°F. To make the crust, mix the flour and salt. Cut in the butter and shortening. Stir in the egg yolk. Add the cold water, 1 tablespoon at a time, to form the dough into a ball. Chill. Roll out and place in a high-sided 9-inch quiche pan with removable sides. Pierce with a fork. Bake for 7 to 9 minutes, or until lightly toasted. Cool. Reduce the oven temperature to 350°F.

To make the filling, heat 2 tablespoons of the olive oil in a frying pan and sauté the garlic and onion until transparent, not brown. Remove and set aside.

Add the remaining 2 tablespoons olive oil and sauté the zucchini and green pepper until slightly tender. Combine them with the onion mixture.

In a separate bowl, mix the eggs with the cottage cheese. Stir in the cream cheese and, if necessary, slice with a pastry cutter to break up any lumps. Add the salt, pepper, dill, and nutmeg. Then add the onion mixture, spinach, Parmesan cheese, and cream. Mix well.

Pour into the crust. Bake for 40 minutes, or until the center is set. Remove the sides from the quiche pan and serve hot.

Leg of Lamb Roasted
With White Wine and Herbs
Yield: 6 to 8 servings

6-pound leg of lamb
Salt and freshly
  ground pepper
1½ cups dry white
  wine
½ cup olive oil
4 garlic cloves,
  minced
1 tablespoon dried
  oregano
½ teaspoon dried
  thyme
Juice of 1 lemon

My neighbor, Bob Hewett, was the best kind of country neighbor. He plowed our driveway and showed me how to adjust the idle in my car's engine. He raised chickens and sheep and occasionally treated us to a roasting chicken or a cut of lamb. Bob insisted his bounty should be cooked right away. But I am of the rainy-day school and froze the meat for a special occasion. These days, I am coming around to Bob's view and prefer to use fresh, local lamb when it is available.

* * *

Sprinkle the lamb with salt and pepper. Mix 1 cup of the white wine with the olive oil, garlic, herbs, and lemon juice. Place the lamb in a dish and pour the marinade over. Rub it in well. Transfer the lamb and the marinade to a double plastic bag. Squeeze out all the air and seal with a twist tie. Marinate for several hours or overnight.

Bring the lamb to room temperature. Remove from the marinade and wipe dry. Preheat the oven to 400°F. Insert a meat thermometer in the lamb. Place the lamb in a roasting pan and set in the oven to brown for 15 minutes.

Reduce the oven temperature to 350°. Add the remaining ½ cup wine to the marinade and baste frequently. Roast to the desired degree of doneness. Allow 16 to 18 minutes per pound to reach an internal temperature of 140° (rare); 20 to 25 minutes per pound to reach 160° (medium); and 30 to 35 minutes to reach 170° to 180° (well done).

Allow the lamb to stand for 10 minutes before carving. Slice thinly. Remove the fat from the pan juices. Correct the seasonings and serve the juices on the side.

Mushroom and Potato Casserole *Yield: 4 servings*

1 pound potatoes
½ pound mushrooms
Butter
1 garlic clove,
  chopped
Salt and pepper
⅔ cup light cream
⅔ cup heavy cream
¼ cup water
¼ cup grated
  Parmesan cheese

If your menu calls for potatoes but you want to make them special, try Eugene's casserole. It has the flavor of his native Hungary. This dish goes nicely with a green salad and steak.

* * *

Peel the potatoes and slice thinly. Slice the mushrooms thicker than the potatoes. Using lots of butter, grease a 1½-quart glass baking dish. Sprinkle the garlic on the bottom.

Arrange half the potato slices in overlapping rows on the bottom of the dish. Season with salt and pepper. Arrange a layer of mushrooms on top and season with salt and pepper. Top it off with a layer of potatoes.

Stir together the light cream, heavy cream, and water. Pour on top. Sprinkle with the Parmesan cheese and dot with more butter.

Bake for about 1 hour at 350°F., or until the potatoes are tender and the top is crisp. Remove from the oven and let stand for 5 to 10 minutes. Serve at once.

Food for Thought
Followed by Dinner

It has no name, there are no dues, and no one is in charge. We refer to it as The Book Group, The Meeting, or simply, The Readers. Once a month, we gather to discuss a book and share a potluck supper.

There are twelve of us. Each of us enjoys reading the classics and discovering new writers. The last time any of us met to explore something we read was in college. And that was from three to thirty-five years ago.

It all began when two of us talked about our favorite authors to pass the time on a drive to Boston. My friend is also a writer and editor. She was astonished I had not read John Gardner and I thought everyone had discovered Maxine Hong Kingston.

During the next few months, we talked with friends about organizing a group. Someone stopped talking and set a date. Twelve people arrived with at least twelve apprehensions. I, for one, won't read J. R. R. Tolkien, Barbara Cartland, or George Eliot. But I don't have to worry about those three anymore. Rather, I fear we will run out of time before we read all the other books on our list.

Our first assignment was *The Dogs of March* by Ernest Hebert. The novel's setting is northern New England and the people are our neighbors and ourselves.

The first discussion ran like a car in winter with a bit of water in the gas tank. The talk flowed, halted, and chugged. But we had to test the idea of a book group and each other. The organizer prodded us with her questions about style and characterization. Was Mr. Hebert making fun of all of us? What does Howard Elman's name mean? Where is the town of Darby?

We struggled to find our method. Since then we have read *A Bend in the River* by V. S. Naipaul, *Lying* by Sissela Bok, *The Right Stuff* by Tom Wolfe, and *From Down to the Village* by David Budbill. Also *The Soul of a New Machine* by Tracy Kidder, *The Sound and the Fury* by William Faulkner, and *One Hundred Years of Solitude* by Gabriel Garcia Marquez.

We have begun to respond to each other and each book from any one of our several selves: artist, cabinetmaker, carpenter, teacher, writer, reporter, father, mother, child, divorced or single person.

In the winter, we meet in apartments in the valley. In the summer, we recline in hilltop pastures or on the shores of Lake Skatutakee.

We had to make two rules. First, there is no shoptalk, which excludes, bores, and trivializes. Second, we begin promptly at 4 P.M., because even though it is a Sunday, some people must correct papers or play softball early in the evening. Those who can linger over coffee often do. But no one is cheated of any discussion.

Before we adjourn, we settle the details for the next meeting: the book, the place, the date, and parts of the menu. The host supplies a main dish and beverages. People bring their own wine and beer.

Although we may be slow to talk about a book, we never hesitate to comment about the surprisingly good food.

"Is that basil I taste in these tomatoes?"

"Where do you get the fresh ginger?"

"Do you grow your own sprouts?"

"Indian pudding is supposed to be soupy."

"It's easy to make carrot cake if you use a food processor."

We have shared food that is as diverse as the people who prepare it. Some readers have even developed specialties both in food and in literature. One, for example, has introduced us to the writers of South America. Another likes to explore new American literature.

One cook manages to prepare a spectacular fruit salad in deepest winter. Another has brought making vegetable salads to a great art. I often volunteer to bake bread or dessert, adapting it to the flavor of the day's literature or the mood I am in when I awake that morning.

In any case, one of the best parts of the book group happens weeks away from the meeting. As I read the assigned book and am moved to envy, bewilderment, or joy, it's nice to know there is some place to take my comments.

Nora Kels's Stuffed Mushrooms
Yield: 25 to 35 stuffed mushrooms

1 to 1½ pounds fresh
 large mushrooms
3 tablespoons
 margarine
2 garlic cloves,
 crushed
½ cup sherry or white
 wine
½ to ⅔ cup bread
 crumbs
½ cup grated cheddar
 cheese
1 can (6 ounces) crab
 meat (optional)
⅓ cup sherry

Clean the mushrooms. Carefully break the stems off the caps at the base. Chop the stems finely. Heat the margarine in a frying pan and sauté the mushroom stems with the garlic for 5 minutes.

Turn the heat down. Add the ½ cup sherry or white wine, and simmer for 10 minutes. Add the bread crumbs and grated cheese (and flaked crab meat, if desired) and mix all together. The mixture should be moist enough to stick together. If it is too dry, add a little more sherry.

Preheat the oven to 350°F.

Pack the stuffing into the caps, mounding it up. Place each filled cap in a shallow pan and pour about ⅓ cup sherry or water into the pan. Cover loosely with aluminum foil and bake for 15 minutes.

Then remove the foil, increase the oven heat to 375°, and bake for 5 minutes to brown the tops. Serve warm.

Bill Brock's Stewed Squirrels
Yield: 9 servings

3 squirrels, cleaned
 and quartered
1 quart water
1 teaspoon salt
¼ teaspoon black
 pepper
1 can (16 ounces)
 whole tomatoes
1 medium-size onion,
 chopped
1 bay leaf
½ teaspoon dried
 thyme
2 carrots, chopped
3 potatoes, diced
Steamed rice

When Jim Duncan belonged to our book group, we could always count on him to bring a loaf of banana bread, his specialty. When he hosted the group, he surprised us with a pot of squirrel stew. There are those who say squirrel tastes like rabbit, which in turn tastes like chicken. I, for one, thought Jim's squirrels were more succulent than any chicken raised in a factory. This is Jim's friend's recipe.

* * *

Place all the ingredients, except the rice, in a large pot. Cover and bring to a boil. Reduce the heat to simmer and cook until the meat is tender, about 2½ hours. Remove the bay leaf. Ladle the stew onto steamed rice and serve.

Cynthia's Macaroni and Cheese

Yield: 4 servings

1¼ cups scalded milk
½ cup soft bread crumbs
3 tablespoons butter
1½ cups cooked macaroni
2 tablespoons minced onion
¼ cup chopped olives
2 eggs, well beaten
1 cup grated cheddar cheese
1 teaspoon Worcestershire sauce
½ teaspoon salt
6 tomato slices
Olive slices
Buttered bread crumbs

When Cynthia Georgina managed a New Hampshire radio station, she also hosted a daily interview show. Tune in one day, and you heard all about using a divining rod to locate underground water. Tune in the next day, and you learned how to chart your family tree or your horoscope. Or locate your birth mother. Or make an almond-flavored dessert from China. You never knew. And that was the fun.

Of the following dish, Cynthia says, "This recipe is delicious. The base is custardy and studded with olives and macaroni. I serve it with sliced ham, a salad, and corn muffins.

* * *

Preheat the oven to 375°F.

Pour the milk over the ½ cup soft bread crumbs and butter. Add the macaroni, onion, chopped olives, eggs, cheese, Worcestershire sauce, and salt. Mix thoroughly. Place in a buttered 8-inch baking dish.

Place the dish in a pan of hot water and bake until a knife inserted in the center comes out clean, about 45 minutes. Top with tomato slices, sliced olives, and buttered crumbs. Bake for an additional 5 minutes. Serve hot.

Rum Raisin Copley Squares

Yield: 24 squares

3 tablespoons butter
⅔ cup firmly packed
 brown sugar
1 egg
2 tablespoons light
 molasses
4 teaspoons light rum
½ teaspoon vanilla
 extract
¾ cup unbleached all-
 purpose flour
½ teaspoon baking
 powder
¼ teaspoon salt
¼ teaspoon ground
 cinnamon
⅛ teaspoon ground
 nutmeg
½ cup raisins,
 coarsely chopped
½ cup chocolate chips
Fine dry bread
 crumbs
¼ cup confectioners'
 sugar

How did these cookies get their name? Well, they were square and to me, elegant. So I named them after an elegant place in Boston, Copley Square. The first time I served them, they were still plain raisin squares. After my husband and I were married in front of the fireplace at our home, we invited a few friends and neighbors over for champagne and sweets. When the guests asked for the recipe, I added the name. They have become a favorite at our book discussion gatherings.

* * *

Preheat the oven to 350°F.

Cream the butter and brown sugar until fluffy. Add the egg, molasses, 3 teaspoons of the rum, and the vanilla. Beat until blended.

Sift the flour with the baking powder, salt, cinnamon, and nutmeg. Add to the batter and beat again. Stir in the raisins and the chocolate chips.

Grease an 8-inch square baking dish and dust with the bread crumbs. Spread the batter evenly in the pan and bake for 20 to 22 minutes, until the top feels firm to the touch and the cake begins to shrink from the sides of the pan.

Mix the confectioners' sugar with the remaining 1 teaspoon rum and dribble over the warm cake. Cool the cake in the pan and cut into 24 bars. Store in an airtight tin. These squares freeze well.

Chapter Two

Season of Mud
And Sugar

W hen the snow turns gray and everything else in the world seems to be mud brown, we invest our hopes in amber gold. That's the color of maple syrup, and it flows as the earth begins to thaw.

The sweetness of the maple season is tempered by the fact that the thaw also brings the mud season. As the thaw water rushes down the mountains to the river, our dooryards and unpaved roads are turned to mud. The mud clings to the bottoms of our chain-tread boots. The country roads become deeply rutted, and when our cars get stuck, we wait until a neighbor can pull us out. Occasionally, the roads become impassable for a day or two. But we don't mind.

Paving our road would mean bulldozing the stone fences that line its edges, felling the maple shade trees, and sacrificing the borders of June pinks and wild asters. If squishing through the mud for a few weeks a year is the toll collected for living on a picture-postcard road, I, for one, am glad to pay it.

Sap's Running!
Here Comes the Liquid Gold

It is safe to say that I have been seduced by almost every country craft. I have embraced candle dipping, wine making, peanut growing, and flower drying.

However, I never surrendered to maple madness. Not that I haven't been tempted. I live in a sugar bush — as a stand of maple trees is called — and I am aware that there are gallons of free syrup out there waiting to be tapped.

But I have learned from the stories told by my native and born-again New Hampshire neighbors. Every February, as the sap begins flowing, people confess their single experience with sugaring. They describe boiling down forty-five gallons of sap on an electric kitchen stove until they produced one gallon of syrup.

There is a recurrent theme in these tales. The one-time sugarers never asked themselves nor anyone else where the forty-four gallons of boiled-off moisture would go — until the wallpaper peeled off the walls, and the house was soggy with a humidity worthy of mid-August.

Now I don't dismiss backyard sugaring at all. I just think you can save yourself a lot of time, energy, and wallpaper if you talk to seasoned sugarers before beginning your operation.

In fact, up the Connecticut River from me there is a Dartmouth College professor who has made a second career of backyard sugaring. Noel Perrin has written articles and an entire book of practical advice about harvesting maple sugar.

An abundant supply of firewood and a sugarhouse are a good start. Sugarhouses are more nearly sugar shacks — small rough buildings with wide cracks in the walls for escaping steam.

I prefer to replenish my supply every spring from a small producer. It is reassuring to read the label while feasting on pancakes. The label says, "Sweet Inspiration Pure New Hampshire Maple Syrup. Light Amber Fancy Grade. Boiled on the wood fires at Cook Hill Farm by Francis Sutherland."

As I spoon the last bit of syrup from the plate, I think about Francis and Helen Sutherland, who have been farming for many years in Alstead, New Hampshire, a few towns up the Connecticut River from me. The Sutherlands are warm, generous people who organized the farmers' market in our county.

Listening to the nonproducers grouse about the high price of pure maple syrup is as much a sign of spring as the chickadee's mating call. But sugaring, as the economists say, is labor-intensive, although technology has been introduced at several stages of the long journey from tree to bottle.

Some maple producers now use vacuum pumps to collect sap from the trees and pipe it through plastic hose to the sugarhouse. The liquid is then boiled in an evaporator — a sheet metal pan, often the size of a pool table — until it becomes thick enough for syrup. Both large and small producers usually welcome visitors to their sugarhouses. "There's not a lot you can do while watching the sap boil except shoot the breeze with anyone who comes by," said one.

For the visitor, the sugarhouse is a warm and steamy refuge from the gray, chilly March weather. You can smell the sweet maple in the air long before you approach the shack. Sugaring reminds you that winter is not forever. In fact, the maple harvester races against budding. When the buds break out, the season is finished.

Some commercial producers skip the boiling step altogether. They extract the syrup from the sap using a reverse-osmosis machine and save both time and fuel. On the other hand, there are still people who sugar the way it was done fifty years ago. For these small farmers, the maple season is just one of many adding up to the full measure of the year.

Alfred Despres of Marlborough, New Hampshire, was such a man. Every year about February 28, he hung eight hundred buckets in his sugar bush. To collect the sap, he wore a wooden shoulder yoke that held a pair of buckets. While Alfred boiled, his wife, Bernadette, made maple butter and maple cream candies. She welcomed visitors to the sugarhouse with fragrant coffee and a slice of her maple squash bread. The couple produced about 150 gallons of syrup every year. "By town meeting [the second Tuesday in March], we were always quite busy," Bernadette said.

Alfred liked to point out how the fickle combination of the elements — wind, temperature, sun, and frost — controlled the harvest. While a neighbor might report a gushing run, at the same moment the sap would be just trickling into the Despres buckets.

Like most precious things, maple syrup needs proper care. Store an unopened container at room temperature. To preserve the flavor, an opened container must be stored in the refrigerator. If you have a large amount to store, maple producers suggest pouring the syrup into clean, airtight containers and keeping them in the freezer.

How do you like your maple syrup? Most of the four million gallons produced annually in the United States probably is poured on pancakes. New Hampshire people tell me they like it on their waffles, oatmeal, and vanilla ice cream. They also put it in muffins, fudge, baked squash, and apple crisp.

My friend Ann Couturier Fitz says the best way to enjoy the first run of the season is right in the sugarhouse. "You dip a fresh, warm plain doughnut into maple syrup. There is nothing on earth quite like it."

In Vermont, the maple-syrup-doughnut combination calls for dill pickles on the side to cut the sweetness of the other two.

I asked Ann about the dills. "I don't know about the pickles . . . . Well, that's Vermont," she said.

Maple-Barbecued Ribs

Yield: 4 to 6 servings

3 pounds spareribs
1 cup pure maple
  syrup
2 tablespoons chili
  sauce
2 tablespoons white
  distilled or cider
  vinegar
1 grind black pepper
½ cup chopped onion
2 teaspoons
  Worcestershire
  sauce
1 teaspoon salt
½ teaspoon dry
  mustard
¼ cup brandy
  (optional)

The flavors of maple syrup and pork are especially compatible. The best spareribs I have eaten were served by a woman who raises her own pork and collects her own maple syrup. The following recipe is in the spirit of the ribs my friend served one late-winter afternoon.

* * *

Preheat the oven to 375°F.

Cut the spareribs into serving-size pieces and place in a single layer in a shallow baking pan. Mix the remaining ingredients and pour over the ribs, turning to coat all sides. Bake for 1½ to 2 hours. Turn the pieces and brush with the sauce frequently while baking. The ribs are done when the meat is very tender. Serve hot.

Maple Squash Pie

Yield: 6 to 8 servings

1 tablespoon
  cornstarch
⅓ cup sugar
½ teaspoon ground
  cinnamon
½ teaspoon ground
  nutmeg
¼ teaspoon salt
1 cup cooked winter
  squash or pumpkin
  purée
1⅓ cups pure maple
  syrup
½ cup milk
1 tablespoon melted
  butter
2 eggs, beaten
1 unbaked 9-inch or
  10-inch pie shell
Whipped cream
  (optional)

Preheat the oven to 450°F.

Stir together the cornstarch, sugar, cinnamon, nutmeg, and salt. Beat into the squash. Add the maple syrup, milk, and butter and mix. Stir in the beaten eggs. Pour into the pie shell. Bake for 15 minutes. Lower the heat to 325° and continue baking for 40 minutes, or until a knife inserted 1 inch from the center comes out clean.

Remove from the oven and allow to set for at least 10 minutes. Serve warm or cooled. Top with whipped cream, if desired.

Maple Walnut Mousse

Yield: 4 to 6 servings

1 envelope (1
   tablespoon)
   unflavored gelatin
¼ cup cold water
3 eggs, separated
1 cup pure maple
   syrup
¾ cup heavy cream
1 cup chopped
   walnuts

Fashions in mousse change as surely as fashions in skirts. Even timid chefs turned out bowl after bowl of chocolate mousse after the food processor was introduced. Then, for a few months, white chocolate mousse dominated the dessert menus at trendy restaurants. I don't know whether maple mousse was ever a fad, but I do know it holds its own among airy desserts.

* * *

Soften the gelatin in the cold water. Set aside.

In the top of a double boiler, beat the egg yolks until thick and lemon colored. Beat in the maple syrup. Place the maple-egg mixture over hot water, and cook and stir until slightly thickened. Add the gelatin and stir until dissolved. Remove from the heat and chill until the mixture becomes syrupy. Beat until fluffy — about 5 minutes with an electric beater.

In a separate bowl, beat the egg whites until stiff and carefully fold them into the maple syrup mixture. Refrigerate the mousse until firm — 3 to 4 hours.

Just before serving, whip the cream. Fold the nuts into the whipped cream and serve on top of the mousse.

Maple Butter

Yield: 5 ounces

½ cup butter, softened
2 tablespoons pure
    maple syrup
1 tablespoon brandy

This flavored butter is a nice way to say, "I am glad I know you." Pack it in a fancy little jar and add a tag with the recipe. Don't be tempted to use a substitute for the butter or *the maple syrup.*

* * *

Whip the butter, maple syrup, and brandy together. Pack into a crock, if desired, and store in the refrigerator. Serve on sweet potatoes, winter squash, or hot muffins.

Agnes's Ever-Ready Bran Muffins

Yield: 48 muffins

2 cups raisins
2 cups boiling water
5 cups All-Bran cereal
1½ cups sugar plus
    1½ cups maple
    syrup, molasses, or
    honey, or 3 cups
    sugar
1 cup vegetable oil
4 eggs, beaten
1 quart buttermilk
5 cups unbleached all-
    purpose flour
5 teaspoons baking
    soda

Having 4 batches of ready-to-be-baked bran muffin batter in the refrigerator is in the same luxury category as a coffee maker timed to wake you up as it brews. Agnes's version of this high-fiber muffin makes 4 quarts of batter that will keep for 6 weeks in the refrigerator. Don't freeze the batter, she warns.

* * *

Mix the raisins and boiling water with 2 cups of the cereal. Set aside.

In a large bowl, mix the sweetener and oil. Then stir in the eggs, buttermilk, and remaining 3 cups cereal.

Mix the flour and baking soda and add to the egg-buttermilk mixture. Add the bran-raisin mixture. Refrigerate in jars.

Each quart makes 12 muffins. To bake, spoon the batter into greased muffin tins. Fill two-thirds full. Bake in a preheated 400°F. oven for 15 to 20 minutes. Cool slightly before removing from pans. Serve warm or cooled.

Maple Squash Bread

Yield: 2 loaves

½ cup pure maple
  syrup
1¼ cups firmly
  packed brown sugar
1 cup salad oil
3 eggs, slightly beaten
2 cups cooked winter
  squash or pumpkin
  purée
3 cups unbleached all-
  purpose flour
1¼ teaspoons baking
  soda
½ teaspoon baking
  powder
2 teaspoons ground
  cinnamon
1 teaspoon ground
  nutmeg
1 teaspoon ground
  cloves

The nice thing about this recipe is that it makes 2 loaves. That means if you are making a loaf for yourself, it is no more work to make another to share.

* * *

Preheat the oven to 325°F.

In a large bowl, mix together the maple syrup, brown sugar, oil, and eggs. Beat in the squash purée.

Stir together the flour, baking soda, baking powder, and spices. Add to the squash mixture and stir until blended.

Pour the batter into 2 greased and floured 5-inch by 9-inch by 3-inch loaf pans. Bake for 1 hour, or until the loaves are lightly browned and a toothpick inserted in the center comes out clean.

Cool for 10 minutes in the pans; then turn out onto racks and cool.

Note: Vary the recipe by adding ⅔ cup chopped walnuts or raisins.

Sugar-on-Snow

When I discovered the maple treat called sugar-on-snow, my longing for the toffee of my youth disappeared.

You make sugar-on-snow by heating maple syrup to 240°F. and pouring it on a pie tin packed with clean snow. The syrup hardens as it touches the snow and becomes a sticky toffee. To eat, twirl the mass on a fork as you would spaghetti. Stray golden strands will probably web your nose and chin, but that is part of the pleasure.

Yankee natives who have moved far away from a source of fresh snow have been known to satisfy their urge for this early spring treat by pouring mail-order maple syrup over crushed ice and savoring the sweet while sitting on their condo terrace, watching the sun set over the Gulf of Mexico. But the rest of us are content to visit a sugarhouse or attend a sugar-on-snow supper at one of the village churches. The supper is one of the many seasonal fund raisers marking everything from harvest to town meeting.

Some years, the breaking of bread at the town meeting supper is strained by the split between those who want an addition on the schoolhouse and those who press for a new fire truck. But most such rifts begin to mend by the sugar-on-snow supper, as townspeople acknowledge feelings change as surely as the seasons.

Although women are often the cooks for the community meals, the men of Westmoreland, New Hampshire, put on the sugar-on-snow supper for nearly a decade.

People who come to Westmoreland for supper can feast on more than mere food. The town is the site of an exquisite meetinghouse built in 1762 on the top of a hill overlooking the fertile Connecticut River valley. Every time I come upon the Park Hill Meeting House, I am filled with wonderment for its architect and builders.

I am grateful, too, for those who care enough about the building to preserve it for passersby like me. The meetinghouse can be enjoyed at any season, but I think I like it best when its whiteness contrasts with the emerald hues of early summer.

The men's sugar-on-snow supper raised money for a variety of projects, including the maintenance of the meetinghouse. However, the men's supper tradition ended when several of the cooks moved away. But Westmoreland is a supper kind of town, and people still travel to the strawberry supper and the annual Fourth of July chicken barbecue sponsored by the fire department.

You can usually count on chickens for your barbecue and strawberries for your supper, but you can't always expect a supply of snow for your dessert. Talbot Hood, town moderator, recalled one mild year when the men had to cross the river to Vermont to scoop up enough snow to make the dessert.

Tal collected the following recipes from the men's supper menu. Baked beans, of course, is a traditional Saturday-night supper dish in New England. The maple glaze is a simple way to make a baked ham special. The dinner rolls originated in Boston's Parker House where they are still served. Steaming coffee is served with the maple dessert and a sing-along is a convivial finish to the evening.

If you are having your own sugar-on-snow supper, remember that a gallon of the liquid gold will sweeten about sixty guests.

Maple Baked Beans

Yield: 12 servings

**1 pound dried navy
    pea beans**
Water
½ cup chopped onion
**½ to ¾ cup pure
    maple syrup**
1 teaspoon salt
**2 tablespoons dry
    mustard**
**1 teaspoon ground
    ginger**
**6 bacon strips, cut
    into 1-inch slices**

There are 2 main schools of sweetening when it comes to baked beans — you prefer either maple syrup or molasses. The following recipe is of the first school, while the next recipe is of the second. Just to tighten up the game, a third school has emerged lately. It suggests using ½ cup orange marmalade.

* * *

Place the beans in a 2½-quart casserole or bean pot. Cover with water and let soak overnight. Drain. Place the beans in a large saucepan, cover with fresh water, and bring to a boil. Lower the heat and simmer for 1 to 1½ hours, or until the beans are tender and the skins have burst.

Drain the beans and reserve the water. To 1 cup of the reserved water, add the onion, maple syrup, salt, mustard, and ginger. Place the beans in a casserole or bean pot and stir in the maple mixture. Add the bacon. Add enough reserved water to cover the beans.

Bake for 6 hours at 325°F. Stir occasionally during the cooking and add the reserved water, ½ cup at a time, if the beans appear to be sticking to the crock or are dry. Serve hot.

Note: To vary the flavor, add ¼ cup coffee or ¼ cup bourbon to the beans. Also, the beans can be made in a slow cooker. Use the low setting, keep covered, and cook for 10 to 12 hours.

Alonzo Hudson's Baked Beans

Yield: 10 servings

2 pounds dried soldier
  beans
Water
1 teaspoon baking
  soda
1 small onion, sliced
½ to 1 pound salt
  pork
1 cup firmly packed
  brown sugar
¼ cup molasses
⅓ cup pure maple
  syrup
2 teaspoons salt
1½ teaspoons dry
  mustard
½ teaspoon ground
  ginger

Baked beans became the Saturday-night special throughout New England because servile work, such as cooking, was forbidden on Sunday. The Yankee cook provided for both days by baking a large pot of beans. The Pilgrims might be surprised that baked beans are still a Saturday favorite in New England. They might also be astonished at the sight of their descendants scurrying about the shopping malls on a Sunday afternoon.

* * *

Soak the beans overnight in water to cover. In the morning, add the baking soda and boil until the beans sound hollow when stirred but are not mushy. Drain in a colander and rinse with cold water.

Place the onion in the bottom of the bean pot. Add half the beans. Then cut the salt pork through just to the rind in 1-inch squares. Add to the pot. Pour the remainder of the beans on top of the pork. Then pour the brown sugar, molasses, and maple syrup on top of the beans. Mix the salt, mustard, and ginger with enough hot water to make a paste, and pour over all.

Cover the beans with cold water. Bake in a 250° to 300°F. oven for 6 to 8 hours. Add water as necessary to keep the beans moist. Serve hot.

Ken Stewart's Glazed Ham

Yield: Glaze for 1 whole ham

Steep 10 to 12 whole cloves in ½ cup maple syrup for 1 week.

When you are ready to bake the ham, preheat the oven to 325°F. Insert a meat thermometer into the ham, set the ham on a rack in a shallow pan, and bake. For a 10-pound to 15-pound ham, allow 18 to 20 minutes per pound; for a 5-pound to 7-pound ham, allow about 20 minutes per pound.

About 20 minutes before the end of the ham's baking time, check the thermometer for the internal temperature of the meat. If you are heating a ham that is already fully cooked, spread the glaze over the ham when the internal temperature reaches 130°. Continue baking for about 20 more minutes or until internal temperature reaches 140°.

If you are baking a cook-before-eating ham, spread the glaze on the ham when the internal temperature reaches 140° and continue baking until the temperature reaches 160°.

Let the ham stand for 10 minutes before carving.

Church Supper Coleslaw

Yield: 12 servings

**6 cups shredded
  cabbage**
1 cup shredded carrot
**¼ cup diced green
  pepper**
**1 medium-size onion,
  chopped**
1 cup diced celery
1 cup mayonnaise
2 tablespoons sugar
**2 tablespoons white
  distilled vinegar**
**1 teaspoon prepared
  mustard**
**1 teaspoon celery
  seeds**
**Cherry tomatoes
  (optional)**

The Dutch introduced coleslaw to America. Cabbage is the essential ingredient, and the Dutch settlers grew it in their kitchen gardens in what was then New Amsterdam. The word coleslaw comes from the Dutch, koolsla, *meaning cabbage salad. Coleslaw by any name can be varied by adding raisins, chopped nuts, or bits of fruit, such as apple or pineapple.*

* * *

Toss the cabbage, carrot, green pepper, onion, and celery.

In a separate bowl, combine the mayonnaise, sugar, vinegar, mustard, and celery seeds and mix thoroughly. Toss the dressing lightly with the vegetables. Chill for 2 to 3 hours before serving. Place cherry tomatoes around the edge of a serving bowl, if desired.

Note: You can easily substitute heavy cream, sour cream, or plain yogurt for part of the mayonnaise.

Glen Pfistner's
Parker House Rolls

Yield: 3 dozen rolls

1 package (1 scant
    tablespoon) active
    dry yeast
¼ cup warm water
1 cup milk
¼ cup lard or butter
¼ cup sugar
1 teaspoon salt
1 egg, beaten
3¼ cups unbleached
    all-purpose flour

These yeast rolls originated in the Parker House, a hotel and restaurant in Boston. The city is the banking center of New England, so it is fitting that the rolls are shaped like tiny purses.

* * *

Dissolve the yeast in the warm water and set it aside.

Warm the milk, add the lard or butter, and stir until it dissolves. In a large mixing bowl, combine the sugar, salt, and milk-shortening mixture. Stir and add the egg.

Then add the yeast mix and stir well. Add 1½ cups of the flour and stir. Add the balance of the flour and stir. Let the mixture rise in the bowl until doubled in bulk, 45 to 50 minutes. Punch it down.

Remove the dough from the bowl. On a lightly floured surface, roll out the dough to a thickness of approximately ⅓ inch. Cut out circles of dough with a tumbler. Spread the tops of the circles with butter. Fold in half. In a greased 9-inch by 13-inch pan, make 4 rows of rolls, 9 in a row. Let rise until doubled in size.

Preheat the oven to 425°F. Bake for 10 minutes. Reduce the heat to 375° and bake for 5 to 10 minutes longer. Remove the rolls from the pan and cool on a rack.

Boston Baked Brown Bread

Yield: 2 loaves

1½ cups unbleached
all-purpose flour
1 cup whole wheat
flour
1 cup cornmeal
2½ teaspoons baking
soda
1 cup raisins
⅓ cup melted
shortening
1 egg, beaten
2 cups buttermilk or
sour milk
¾ cup molasses

Boston brown bread and baked beans are as married as the ingredients in the New Orleans specialty, red beans and rice. The cooks who created these pairings knew more about nutrition than we thought. The grain in the bread or rice combined with the navy beans or red kidney beans creates a high-quality protein that is surprisingly low in cost.

* * *

Preheat the oven to 350°F.

Stir together the flours, cornmeal, baking soda, and raisins. In a separate bowl, combine the remaining ingredients. Add to dry ingredients, stirring just enough to mix.

Turn into 2 well-greased 5-inch by 9-inch by 3-inch loaf pans. Bake for 45 to 50 minutes. Cool for 10 minutes in the pans, then turn out onto cooling racks. Serve warm with butter.

Note: To sour fresh milk, add 1 tablespoon vinegar to each cup of milk; let stand for 5 minutes and then stir.

To vary the recipe, substitute 1 cup graham or rye flour for the whole wheat flour.

Cecil Cunningham's Doughnuts

Yield: Approximately 2 dozen doughnuts

1 egg
1 cup sugar
2 tablespoons melted
   shortening
1 cup sour milk
2½ cups unbleached
   all-purpose flour
1 teaspoon baking
   powder
1 teaspoon baking
   soda
½ teaspoon ground
   cinnamon
½ teaspoon ground
   nutmeg
½ teaspoon ground
   ginger
½ teaspoon salt
Oil, for frying

These cake-style doughnuts are lightly spiced and best served warm. Correct temperature is a must in deep-fat frying. Use an electric deep-fat fryer for best results. For safety's sake, declare the kitchen off-limits to children and pets until the frying is finished and the fat is cooled.

* * *

Beat the egg; add the sugar, shortening, and sour milk. Sift together the flour, baking powder, baking soda, spices, and salt. Combine with the wet ingredients and mix well.

On a lightly floured surface, roll out the dough to a thickness of approximately ⅓ inch. Cut the dough with a floured doughnut cutter and fry for 3 minutes per side in hot (375°F.) oil. Drain on paper towels and serve warm.

Have Original Recipe, Will Travel to State Cook-off

When Hilda Parsons of Bennington, New Hampshire, went to the National Chicken Cooking Contest one July in Ocean City, Maryland, she returned to our corner of the state $4,000 richer.

I was rooting for Hilda because I was just three skillets away from winning the state cooking contest myself.

It all began during the depths of mud season when the idea of spending a few days in Ocean City cooking chicken seemed like a pleasant escape. I had been looking through a book of chicken contest winners and decided I could create a recipe as good as any in the book. Most of the recipes were variations on familiar themes. They did carry some novel names, but I could make up a name, too.

The next step was making up a recipe. I had to use chicken, and I wanted to include New Hampshire maple syrup.

A check of my cookbook collection revealed a popular way to prepare chicken is cooking it in barbecue sauce. Such sauces include catsup and a sweetener such as honey. I studied a dozen recipes and came up with a workable formula for "Sugarbush Spring Chicken."

I tested my formula on two occasions — both of which were last-minute invitations to dinner. You should know that if your dinner guests like to poke around in the kitchen, the sight of a catsup-based sauce is not very promising. But the resulting dish is quite good for a very easy oven-barbecued chicken.

After I mailed my recipe to Washington in late March, I forgot about the contest until one Thursday in late May, when a woman called to invite me to cook my chicken in Penacook on Saturday.

"Your recipe is among the five state finalists," she said. "Can you bring a chicken and whatever else you need and be at the cook-off at nine-thirty in the morning?"

"Wait a minute," I said. "What do you mean whatever else I need?"

"Well, the state people will provide the stove. And they will have aprons for two of you."

Assembling a kitchen-to-go was the most challenging part of the contest. As I filled a picnic hamper with saucepans, baking pans, chicken, a timer, and maple syrup, my husband asked, "Are you sure they will provide the stove?"

Finding Merrimack Valley High School (as opposed to Merrimack High School) was the second challenge. Everything else, as they say, was a piece of chicken.

The contestants arrived at 9:30 A.M. In the New Hampshire Chicken Cooking Contest, promptness doesn't count. A fifth contestant never appeared. Perhaps he or she is still wondering how to haul a stove to whichever of the two Merrimack high schools.

The cutthroat atmosphere at national cooking contests is legendary and understandable. A flick of the pepper mill can make the difference between $10,000 and $4,000. Fortunately, the atmosphere at the Merrimack Valley High School was quite congenial.

Orrin Wilson (Chicken 'N Apple Stuffing) and Mrs. Parsons (Chicken Breast Piquant) were seasoned veterans of cooking contests. They reviewed contests of other years. Mr. Wilson explained how he comes up with a name first and then works out the recipe. Mrs. Parsons fretted she would not have enough time for a necessary thirty minutes of marinating. Judith Larkin of Nashua chatted as she unpacked the sixteen ingredients of her chicken curry.

By 10:00 A.M., the state officials and the judges had arrived. We never laid eyes on the judges; they were secluded in a sewing classroom.

At the most, my chicken recipe takes ten minutes of preparation and sixty minutes of baking. Once my dish was in the oven, I relaxed and enjoyed the aromas of such diverse flavors as brandy, walnuts, apples, coriander, and cardamom. My chicken was the first one finished. It was taken in to the judges and came back soon, with a few bites missing from the bird.

The contestants sampled each dish after the judges had tasted them. I liked Judy Larkin's Chicken Curry best. But I thought Orrin Wilson's chicken with stuffing would win. We washed our dishes and repacked our hampers while waiting for the judges to decide.

New Hampshire Department of Agriculture official Roy Howard told us there was not much difference in the total points awarded to each of us. Then he declared Hilda Parsons the winner. The other contestants hugged her and shook her hand, and she cried.

When Mrs. Parsons took second place in Ocean City, she was just as surprised. Contest officials urged her to telephone the good news home to New Hampshire at their expense.

"Who would I call at 11 o'clock at night?" she asked. "My husband is in bed by then. In New Hampshire, we go to bed early."

Mrs. Parsons's
Chicken Breast Piquant
Yield: 4 servings

2 broiler-fryer
   chicken breasts,
   halved, boned, and
   skinned
1 can (8 ounces)
   crushed pineapple
   in unsweetened
   juice
1 can (6 ounces)
   frozen limeade,
   thawed
1½ ounces light rum
3 whole cloves
⅓ cup unbleached all-
   purpose flour
2 teaspoons salt
¼ cup cooking oil
⅓ cup slivered
   almonds
Hot buttered rice
   (optional)

On a hard surface, pound the chicken with a meat mallet to ½-inch thickness.

In a shallow bowl, make the marinade by mixing the pineapple and its juice, the limeade, rum, and cloves. Add the chicken, turning to coat. Cover and marinate at room temperature for 30 minutes; remove the chicken and drain, reserving the marinade.

In a shallow dish, mix the flour and salt. Add the chicken, a piece at a time, dredging to coat well.

Heat the oil in a frying pan to a medium temperature. Add the chicken and cook, turning frequently, for about 10 minutes, or until brown on all sides.

Remove the chicken and place in a single layer in a large, shallow, greased baking pan. Pour the reserved marinade over the chicken; sprinkle with the almonds.

Bake, uncovered, at 400°F., basting twice, for about 25 minutes, or until a fork can be inserted in the chicken with ease.

To serve, place the chicken on a serving platter and pour the sauce over the chicken. Serve with hot buttered rice, if desired.

Orrin Wilson's
Chicken 'N Apple Stuffing

Yield: 4 servings

Chicken

**1 broiler-fryer
  chicken, cut into
  parts**
⅓ cup butter
**1 tablespoon brown
  sugar**
**1 tablespoon white
  distilled or cider
  vinegar**
1 teaspoon salt
⅛ teaspoon pepper
**⅛ teaspoon dried
  oregano**
**⅛ teaspoon ground
  thyme**
1 garlic clove, minced

Stuffing

**4 cups toasted bread
  cubes**
1 cup chopped celery
**¼ cup peeled,
  chopped apple**
**¼ cup peeled,
  chopped cucumber**
¼ cup chopped onion
**2 tablespoons
  chopped walnuts**

Place the chicken, skin side up, in a single layer in a medium-size baking pan.

In a small saucepan, melt the butter over medium heat. Add the brown sugar, vinegar, and seasonings; stir and pour over the chicken. Bake, uncovered, at 400°F., basting twice, for 40 minutes.

In a large bowl, mix the stuffing ingredients together. Remove the chicken from the oven; drain the drippings from the baking pan, reserving ⅓ cup. Pour the reserved pan drippings over the bread cube mixture; toss lightly to mix.

Place the stuffing around the chicken in the baking pan. Return to the oven and bake for 25 minutes longer, or until a fork can be inserted into a chicken piece with ease. Serve hot.

Judy Larkin's Chicken Curry

Yield: 4 servings

¼ cup cooking oil
1 broiler-fryer
  chicken, cut into
  parts and skinned
2 cups chopped onion
2 garlic cloves,
  minced
1½ tablespoons
  grated fresh ginger
  root
1 tablespoon paprika
1½ teaspoons
  coriander seeds
1 teaspoon salt
1 teaspoon ground
  turmeric
1 teaspoon ground
  cumin
½ teaspoon ground
  cardamom
¼ teaspoon ground
  cinnamon
¼ teaspoon black
  pepper
⅛ teaspoon ground
  cloves
1 carton (8 ounces)
  plain yogurt
6 tablespoons tomato
  paste
Cooked rice

In a large frying pan, heat the oil to a medium temperature. Add the chicken and cook it for about 10 minutes, or until brown on all sides. Remove the chicken and set aside.

In the same frying pan, make a sauce by sautéing the onion and garlic for about 5 minutes, or until brown. Add the remaining seasonings and mix well; stir in yogurt and tomato paste. Return the chicken to the frying pan, turning to coat with the sauce. Cover and simmer over low heat, stirring occasionally, for about 35 minutes, or until a fork can be inserted into a chicken piece with ease. Serve with any variety of hot rice.

Sugarbush Spring Chicken

Yield: 4 servings

1 broiler-fryer
   chicken, cut into
   parts
¼ cup butter
1 large onion,
   chopped
1 garlic clove, minced
⅔ cup catsup
⅓ cup white distilled
   vinegar
¼ cup pure maple
   syrup
2 teaspoons dry
   mustard
1 teaspoon salt
1 teaspoon ground
   ginger

Place the chicken, skin side up, in a single layer in a large, shallow, greased baking pan.

To make the sauce, melt the butter in a medium-size saucepan over low heat. Add the onion and garlic and sauté for about 5 minutes, or until the onion is translucent. Add the remaining ingredients and stir. Heat to boiling and pour over the chicken.

Bake, uncovered, at 350°F. basting occasionally, for 1 hour, or until a fork can be inserted into a chicken piece with ease. Serve hot.

Not for the Birds Only

Toward the end of winter, I begin to wonder who is in charge: me or the birds. At this season, my dooryard is ankle-deep in sunflower seed hulls, and every creature crossing my threshold tracks in yet another pound of empties.

I admit I feed the birds sunflower seeds all winter long. But they won't do their part and dispose of the wrappers properly. No. They just feast on the kernels and toss the hulls on my lawn.

I considered raising the issue at the next tenants' meeting, but you know how the birds are. The blue jays would blame the chickadees and the chickadees would point a wing at the evening grosbeaks.

Thus, when the snow recedes, I rake the hulls and dig them into the garden, grumbling all the time at the birds. As I turn the soil over, I resolve to plant enough seeds for me and the birds. Even though the sun is warming the spot between my shoulder blades, I can still feel the weight of those five-pound supermarket bags of birdseed as I struggle up winter's icy path to the house. It would make more sense to grow a season's supply in this very garden, I tell myself.

And every year, I do raise enough sunflower seeds. But I am a weakling and let the birds harvest the seeds on the stalk. I like their company as I harvest my string beans and tomatoes.

Now you would think a chickadee gathering lunch from the head of a flower the size of a pie plate would grab any seed and fly away. Instead, as the birds pluck each seed they form a mosaic, reminding me of the fastidious person who eats corn on the cob one row at a time — from left to right. I marvel at whatever tells the jays and the nuthatches to harvest their food in an orderly design from a flower holding hundreds of seeds.

And if you are wondering how many seeds there are on the head of a sunflower, you may be interested to know the record is held by a giant Russian variety that has produced at last count one thousand seeds on a single flower.

Both the seeds and the oil are important foodstuffs in Russia, the Balkans, and the Middle East. In the *souks* of Jerusalem, unshelled seeds are sold by the kilo. I recall my surprise when I first saw people snacking on what I regarded as birdseed as they strolled along the marketplace. The men — now that I think about it many women wore veils — cracked the hulls with their teeth, spit them out, and then chewed the kernels.

But now I know better and I buy the seeds for people food at a natural foods store where they cost about half the price of other nuts. I prefer the unsalted, untoasted seeds sold in bulk by weight.

Nutritionally, sunflower kernels are rich in potassium, phosphorus, and vitamin B6. Sunflower oil is high in unsaturated fats, making it a good choice for people who are concerned about controlling cholesterol. The oil has a pleasant, mild taste and makes a light dressing for vegetable salads.

I like to use the seeds in breads and cakes, salads, vegetables, and fish. If you add almonds or sesame seeds to a favorite dish, consider substituting sunflower seeds for a change.

For a richer taste, toast the seeds. Spread them in a shallow pan and place the pan in a 300°F. oven. Stir now and again. Toasting takes between 20 and 30 minutes.

Growing sunflower seeds is easy. The seeds sprout and thrive almost anywhere. If there is a drought, the deep roots find their own water. The pennies and minutes you invest in planting pay off handsomely in big gold blossoms.

If you have any leftover seeds from the winter birdfeed supply, you can plant a handful of them. Sow the seeds directly into the ground about the time you sow beans and plant the tomato and pepper seedlings. Be sure to plant the sunflowers on the north side of the flower or vegetable patch because the tall plants tend to shade their neighbors. You can harvest about one half pound of seed from each plant.

If you are raising sunflowers for a seed crop, be aware there are two varieties. The large striped gray seeds are easy to hull, making them good food for people and birds. Mammoth, Sunbird Hybrid, and Sundak are typical gray-seeded sunflower varieties.

The small black seeds are grown for birdseed and oil. Oilseed and Hybrid 894 are two varieties available for the home garden.

If you are serious about harvesting the seeds, be ready to cut the heads as soon as they show a brownish tinge. Cut each head from the plant, leaving a twelve-inch length of stalk for a handle. Thread a string through the handle and hang the heads to dry in a warm, dry attic or garage.

Some gardeners slipcover the heads with cheesecloth to prevent bird raids. But climbing a ladder to get to the top of a twelve-foot-high sunflower and draping the blossom with cloth is not my idea of enjoying a late-summer afternoon.

When your seeds are ready for threshing, stretch one-half-inch hardware cloth over a bucket or a barrel, and as you rub the head over the cloth, the seeds will drop inside.

Or take my advice and surrender the entire crop to the winged ones. I feel they have earned their lunch by controlling the mosquitoes and black flies that chew me and the beetles of all kinds that chew my plants.

All I want is the pleasure of lying on my chaise longue for at least one afternoon, watching the bright yellow flowers as they turn their heads to follow the path of the sun.

Maybe this was the magic the Incas believed the sunflowers possessed.

Breast of Lamb
With Fruited Rice Stuffing

Yield: 6 servings

**4 pounds breast of
   lamb, cut into 6
   portions
Flour
Salt
Pepper
2 tablespoons oil
1 onion, sliced
1 cup dry white wine
   or broth
3 cups cooked rice
1 Granny Smith
   apple, diced
½ cup chopped dried
   apricots or prunes
⅓ cup chopped green
   onions and tops
1 tablespoon fresh
   lemon juice
½ cup sunflower
   seeds**

White wine, lamb, sunflower seeds, and fruit combine in this special breast of lamb.

* * *

Preheat the oven to 350°F.

Dust the lamb pieces with flour, salt, and pepper. Heat the oil in a large skillet and brown the lamb on both sides.

Place the sliced onion on the bottom of a 9-inch by 13-inch baking pan. Add the wine. Place half the lamb pieces, cavity side up, on top of the onions.

In a medium-size mixing bowl, combine the remaining ingredients. Spoon the rice mixture over the lamb. Place the remaining lamb on top. Cover with aluminum foil. Bake for 1½ to 2 hours, or until tender.

Remove to a serving platter. Spoon any pan juices over the lamb and serve.

Sunflower-Spinach Surprise

Yield: 12 servings

4 jars (6 ounces each)
marinated
artichoke hearts
3 packages (10 ounces
each) frozen
chopped spinach,
thawed and
drained
½ cup butter, softened
2 packages (8 ounces
each) cream cheese,
softened
¾ cup dry white wine
½ cup grated
Parmesan cheese
¼ cup sunflower
seeds

*One of the beauties of this dish is that you must
make and assemble it a day ahead. Before you
do that, allow ample time for the spinach to thaw
and the cheese to soften. Get all of this behind
you and forget about making dinner.*

*At dinner time, make a salad, heat some
bread, pour some white wine, and serve this dish
— a simple but satisfying supper.*

* * *

Drain the artichokes and arrange them in the
bottom of a greased 9-inch by 13-inch baking
and serving dish. Top with the thawed spinach.

Cream the butter and the cream cheese together. Add the wine gradually and stir until the
mixture is creamy. You can use a food processor
for this step. Pour the mixture over the spinach.
Sprinkle with Parmesan cheese and top with
sunflower seeds. Cover and refrigerate for 24
hours.

Preheat the oven to 350°F.

Bake the casserole for 35 to 45 minutes, or
until lightly browned and bubbly. Cut into
squares and serve.

Rice Pilaf with Sunflower Seeds

Yield: 6 servings

3 tablespoons olive oil
1 cup uncooked rice
½ cup chopped onion
½ teaspoon salt
⅛ teaspoon black
pepper
½ teaspoon dried
oregano
2 cups chicken or beef
stock
⅓ cup sunflower
seeds
1 tablespoon chopped
fresh parsley

*When the price of pine nuts climbed past the
price I was willing to pay, I began substituting
sunflower seeds in some of my favorite recipes.*

* * *

Heat 2 tablespoons of the olive oil in a 2-quart
saucepan. Add the rice and stir constantly until
the rice is golden brown. Add the onion, salt,
pepper, oregano, and stock. Bring to a boil, lower the heat, cover, and simmer for 14 to 17 minutes, or until the liquid is absorbed.

Heat the remaining 1 tablespoon olive oil
in a small saucepan. Stir in the seeds and sauté
until just lightly browned. Stir the seeds and
parsley into the rice. Serve.

Carrot Sunflower Seed Cake

Yield: 9 servings

2 eggs
½ cup honey
¾ cup vegetable oil
¼ cup plain yogurt
1½ cups firmly
packed grated raw
carrots
½ cup sunflower
seeds
1¼ cups whole wheat
flour
1 teaspoon salt
1 teaspoon baking
soda
1 tablespoon ground
cinnamon

Beatrice Trum Hunter is a friend and a neighbor who lives in a small town in the next county. For 2 decades, she operated an inn where she served her summertime guests healthful, natural foods. In the winter, she wrote books on food and nutrition and lectured. She continues to write and warn consumers about the harmful ingredients in processed foods. Mrs. Hunter is her own best advertisement — she has a trim, energetic body and bright, happy eyes.

Whenever I think about her, 2 things come to mind: her splendidly organized walk-in pantry and this wonderful cake. It needs no icing, Mrs. Hunter says, because that would only "gild the lily."

* * *

Preheat the oven to 300°F.

Beat the eggs and add the honey, oil, and yogurt. Blend well, and then stir in the carrots and seeds.

In another bowl, sift together the flour, salt, baking soda, and cinnamon. Fold these dry ingredients into the carrot mix. Blend well, but do not beat. Pour into a buttered 8-inch by 8-inch pan and bake for about 1 hour.

Remove from the oven and cool until the edges separate from the pan. Carefully turn out onto a cake cooling rack.

Note: You can double the recipe and store 1 cake in the freezer. The cake freezes well.

Chapter Three

Budding

W hen spring comes to northern New England and drapes the trees with yellow-green lace, my thoughts turn to free food. That's the food that nature offers us just for the picking. Of course, you have to know what you are doing. For reasons of her own, nature keeps some poisonous things in her pantry, which is why I pick only what I know.

That boils down to dandelion leaves and day lily shoots. I let others stalk the wild asparagus, purslane, and wintercress. Although I know what a fiddlehead looks like, even my best friends won't reveal the site of their secret patch.

Out in the garden, we till, fertilize, plant, and mulch. As we put in the carrots, lettuce, radishes, and onions, we are already anticipating the salads of early July. Meanwhile, the black flies feast on us. We return to the house and rub on stinking but effective fly dope. The flies still swarm above our heads, but they don't bite.

All it takes is one torrid day in May, and the black flies disappear for a dozen months — leaving us to harvest the asparagus and rhubarb without a single itch.

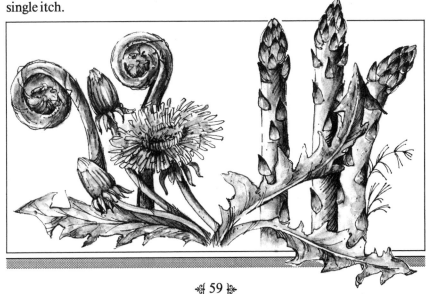

Fiddlehead Fans:
A Secretive Lot

If you think people who fish are a close-mouthed group when it comes to favorite waters, you ought to meet a fiddlehead picker. Fiddlehead pickers make fishers look like gossip columnists.

Fiddleheads are the tender young shoots of the ostrich fern. The coiled sprouts resemble the tip of a fiddle. Cooked gently like asparagus and served with lemon butter, fiddleheads are one of the first delicacies of a New England spring.

The official name of the edible fern is *Matteuccia struthiopteris.* I wish I could tell you how to tell an ostrich fern from a Boston or a bracken fern, but I have never succeeded in coming even close to an ostrich fern patch.

Instead, two friends who do harvest the ferns cut me off at the pass every year. They keep their sources a secret and placate me with a bag of fiddleheads delivered to my door early in May. How can I stand there and demand to know where the ferns were picked when I am already mentally dipping these little beauties in melted butter? Does the caviar lover care where the beluga was fished from the Black Sea?

My friends both grew up in Maine, where fiddleheads are ordinary spring fare. When pressed, these reticent Yankees will say they harvested the sprouts "down to the Connecticut River. But you gotta go there by boat. Awful muddy down there this year."

Of course, the Connecticut River's headwaters are in Pittsburg, New Hampshire, and it empties into Long Island Sound at Saybrook, Connecticut — a distance of four hundred miles. Thus, instead of searching the banks of this great river, I settle for enjoying the gift of fiddleheads and occasionally supplementing my supply with a few pounds bought for $.89 each at a little market on Central Square in nearby Keene.

I am consoled by the thought that fiddleheaders are probably saving us from ourselves. In other places, the ferns have been picked nearly to extinction. That is why in Japan it is against the law to harvest them.

I am consoled, too, by the price of fresh fiddleheads in fancy New York food stores. A friend tells me they sell for $5.99 a pound and are grabbed up as soon as they are displayed.

In any case, fiddlehead time is a giddy season in northern New England. The long, harsh winter is over, and the brown mud season is only a memory. The maple trees are covered with lacy yellow buds about to burst.

For us, the fiddlehead is a taste of the forest as it returns to a warm lushness. People say fiddleheads taste like asparagus, artichokes, or mushrooms. I think asparagus is closest in spirit. If you are blessed with an abundance of fiddleheads, you can use them in any recipe calling for asparagus.

To prepare fiddleheads, remove as much of the papery brown fuzz as you can. Rinse several times. Older cookbooks advise cooking fiddleheads for 20 minutes in boiling water. With the emergence of the crisp-tender school of vegetable cookery, we are told to boil fiddleheads for 5 minutes or steam them for 20 minutes. I like to boil them for about 10 minutes.

True fiddlehead lovers prefer their greens served the same way as their lobster — boiled until just tender and bathed in lemon juice and butter.

Some cooks go as far as hollandaise or cheese sauce. In Maine, fiddle-heads are prepared in a thin cream sauce and served on toast. In fact, canning factories in Maine process fiddleheads and ship them to fine food shops all over the country. Alas, canned fiddleheads may be next of kin to canned spinach.

In any event, I enjoy serving them marinated in a tarragon vinaigrette as an hors d'oeuvre to visitors from the city. Like a born-again Yankee, I don't actually mention who picked the fiddleheads. I just sit back and enjoy all the speculation about how it must be to live off the land.

New Hampshire people who do live off the land and practice folk medicine will bottle the fiddlehead broth in anticipation of the poison ivy and insect-biting season. The broth is applied to the skin and is said to take the itch out of the ivy blisters and the sting out of the black fly bites.

If you would rather feast than fiddle away the season, here are a few favorites.

Fiddlehead Lemon Soup

Yield: 6 servings

1 cup fiddleheads
Water
2 quarts chicken stock
Salt
½ cup uncooked rice
2 eggs
½ cup fresh lemon
  juice

Boil the fiddleheads in water to cover for 5 minutes. Drain.

Bring the stock to a boil and add salt to taste. Add the rice, cover, and simmer for 20 minutes.

Beat the eggs with a rotary beater until light and frothy. Continue beating while adding 2 cups of the hot stock to the eggs. Don't stop beating or the eggs will curdle.

When the eggs and broth are well mixed, pour the mixture back into the remaining broth. Beat in the lemon juice, add the fiddleheads, and heat the entire mixture slowly. Do not boil. Serve warm.

Fiddlehead Quiche

Yield: 6 servings

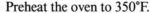

2 cups fiddleheads
1 tablespoon fresh
lemon juice
½ teaspoon salt
¼ teaspoon freshly
ground pepper
3 large eggs
1 unbaked 9-inch pie
shell
1 cup shredded mild
cheddar cheese
¾ cup milk
¾ cup light cream

Preheat the oven to 350°F.

Wash the fiddleheads and steam until just tender, 8 to 10 minutes. Toss the fiddleheads with the lemon juice, salt, and pepper.

Separate one of the eggs. Beat the white and brush it on the bottom of the pie shell. Set the pie shell aside. Combine any remaining egg white with its yolk and the other eggs. Beat slightly.

Sprinkle ¾ cup of the cheese into the pie shell. Arrange the fiddleheads in concentric circles on top of the cheese.

Mix the eggs, milk, and cream. Pour over the fiddleheads. Sprinkle the remaining ¼ cup cheese on top.

Bake for 30 to 35 minutes, or until set and golden brown. Test for doneness by inserting a toothpick in the center of the quiche. When the toothpick comes out clean, the quiche is done. Remove from the oven and let set for 10 minutes before serving.

Note: If you don't have fiddleheads, you can substitute asparagus or zucchini.

Tarragon Fiddleheads

Yield: 6 to 8 servings

4 cups fiddleheads
½ cup olive oil
¼ cup salad oil
¼ cup white distilled
vinegar
¼ teaspoon dried
tarragon
¼ teaspoon sugar
¼ teaspoon dry
mustard
Salt and freshly
ground pepper

Tarragon, an aromatic herb, has an unusual taste that is at once sweet and slightly bitter. I like tarragon in scrambled eggs, sprinkled on baked chicken, and, of course, with asparagus and fiddleheads.

* * *

Boil the fiddleheads in water to cover until crisp-tender — about 5 minutes. Meanwhile, combine the remaining ingredients. Toss the mixture over the hot, drained fiddleheads. Marinate for several hours in the refrigerator. Drain and serve.

Sharon Tisdale's
Deep-Fried Fiddleheads

Yield: 4 servings

5 cups fiddleheads
Water
Oil, for frying
1 cup unbleached all-purpose flour
1½ teaspoons baking powder
½ teaspoon salt
2 eggs, beaten
½ cup milk

Rinse and drain the fiddleheads. Parboil in water to cover for 2 minutes. Drain well.

Heat the oil for deep-frying.

Combine the flour, baking powder, salt, eggs, and milk to make a batter. Drop the fiddleheads into the batter. Stir until covered. Drop into the hot oil and fry until golden. Drain on paper towels and serve.

Dandelions for Wine, Salads, And Fritters

When spring arrives in my backyard, it comes in a yellow burst of forsythia, daffodils, and dandelions. Someone must plant the first two before you can enjoy them. But the cheerful dandelion needs no human hand. It blooms and reseeds itself despite all the effort directed at eradicating this, the gold coin of the plant kingdom.

For decades, the dandelion has been the scourge of suburbia. People dedicate their leisure to producing putting-green lawns. Couples spend evenings and weekends on their knees surgically extracting the plant's deep roots from the earth. Neighborhoods live in fear of the single aigrette that might escape and plant itself in a neighborhood zoned against weeds.

Meanwhile, as children we used to escape to the vacant lots where dandelions were just one treasure among the wildness. We placed the blossoms under each other's chins and predicted wealth or poverty according to the amount of gold reflected on the throat. We made loops of the stems and wove them into chains to drape over our shoulders and bodies. When the season was over, we blew at the seed puffs and as they exploded, we sent a wish with each seed as it took off in the wind.

In recent years, some adults have come to their senses about the food value of dandelions. Food expert Craig Claiborne mentioned dandelion leaves in the same paragraph as radicchio, a very chic wild chicory flown daily to New York from Italy. Mr. Claiborne offered readers of *The New York*

Times a recipe for salmon served with a sauce made of shredded dandelion leaves, clam broth, heavy cream, and caviar.

Country cooks make a less sophisticated but tasty dish of fresh dandelion greens tossed with a warm sweet-and-sour dressing flavored with bacon. New potatoes and corn bread or johnnycakes are served with this spring salad.

A similar dish is served in France, where it is called *salade de pissenlits* and is flavored with salt pork and garlic croutons. The French also make a cream of dandelion green soup that is flavored with onions, garlic, and veal stock.

Oddly enough, the name we use for the plant is from the French *dent de lion*, or tooth of the lion, referring to the saw-toothed shape of the leaves. The French call the plant *pissenlit*.

The greens are grown commercially in France, where a variety has been developed with a flavor superior to that of the wild plant. But, of course, the wild greens are free.

If you want to use the wild leaves for a salad, you must be ready when the leaves are. Harvest them when they are young and tender — when there is simply a rosette of leaves with no stalk in sight. As the stalk and blossom develop, the greens become bitter.

Whether you eat them in a salad or cook them like spinach, dandelion greens are high in vitamin A, iron, calcium, and potassium. Herbalists recommend boiled greens for curing spring fatigue. According to folk medicine, a few servings of the greens will flush away waste deposits that accumulate in the body over the winter.

One of the nice things about this plant is that you can miss one of its acts and catch the next. If, for example, you are not out there in time for the greens, wait a day and you can harvest the tight little buds. Toss them into an omelet or a stir-fry, or pickle them and use them like capers.

Next come the blossoms. You can dip the blossoms in a tempura batter and deep-fry until golden. Or pluck the individual petals from the head and add to a potato or other salad. Or make dandelion wine. Dandelion is considered the best of the simple homemade wines. If you brew it in May, you'll have a bit of sunshine to toast the New Year.

And finally, there are those hardy souls who dig up the roots and make a coffeelike brew by grinding the roasted roots. Sounds like too much work and too little caffeine to me.

If you miss all of the above, pick a dandelion after it has gone to seed, blow hard, and as the seeds scatter, make a wish or many wishes.

Or use the friendly little flower as a clock. In folklore, the dandelion is called the shepherd's clock, because it opens every morning at five and closes again at eight in the evening.

With an eye on a dandelion, you can take a week or two off from watch-winding every spring.

Dandelion Salad

Yield: 4 servings

4 cups tender, young
  dandelion leaves
6 slices bacon
1 tablespoon sugar
¼ cup white distilled
  vinegar
1 hard-cooked egg,
  finely chopped

Here is a traditional recipe for dandelion salad. Chicory or escarole can be substituted for the dandelion greens. My mother used to make this salad with iceberg lettuce when that green was still in favor and roast chicken was considered a luxurious Sunday dinner. Mother's salad is known as wilted lettuce or sweet-and-sour salad.

* * *

Wash and drain the dandelion leaves.

In a skillet, cook the bacon slowly until crisp. Remove the bacon from the skillet and drain on paper towels. Add the sugar and vinegar to the skillet containing the bacon fat. Cook and stir until the sugar is dissolved and the mixture is heated through.

Place the dandelion leaves in a warm bowl and crumble the bacon over the leaves. Add the dressing and toss lightly. Garnish with the chopped egg and serve immediately.

Dandelion Wine

Yield: Approximately 1 gallon

3 quarts dandelion
  blossoms
4 quarts water
3 pounds sugar
Juice and rind of 2
  lemons
Juice and rind of 2
  oranges
1 pound raisins
¼ ounce active dry
  yeast
1 slice toast

Put the blossoms in a large crock. Bring the water to a boil and pour over the blossoms. Let stand for 3 days, stirring once a day.

On the fourth day, pour the contents of the crock into an enamel kettle. Add the sugar and fruit rinds. Boil gently for 1 hour. Then add the fruit juices and raisins. Cool the mixture to lukewarm. Dissolve the yeast in a little warm water and spread the mixture on toast. Float the toast on top of the brew.

Cover the container and let it stand for 6 days. Strain the liquid and pour into sterilized bottles. Cork lightly and do not disturb for about 3 weeks or until the fermentation subsides.

Then press the corks down firmly and store. Let dandelion wine mature for at least 6 months before using.

Dandelion Fritters

Yield: 6 servings

36 dandelion
   blossoms
Oil, for frying
1 cup ice water
1 cup unbleached all-
   purpose flour
½ teaspoon salt
1 egg, beaten

Rinse the dandelion blossoms in cool water and drain thoroughly. Snip off as much of the stem and greenery as possible while leaving the blossom intact. As dandelion greens mature, they become bitter.

Preheat the oil for deep-frying.

Prepare the batter just before frying. The ice water helps create a crisp lacy effect when the blossoms are fried. Stir the water, flour, and salt together. Beat in the egg. Dip the blossoms in batter and deep-fry until golden. Drain on paper towels and serve immediately.

Dandelion Wild Herb Loaf

Yield: 4 to 6 servings

2 cups cooked brown
   rice
2 tablespoons butter
2 eggs, beaten
2 tablespoons
   crumbled dried or
   chopped fresh wild
   mustard
4 cups chopped
   dandelion leaves
⅓ cup chopped
   scallions or 1
   tablespoon chopped
   wild leeks
¼ cup chopped fresh
   wild mint
1 garlic clove, minced
½ cup yogurt or sour
   cream

We know it's spring when the announcement appears for a course on wild edibles. Ty G. Minton is the teacher, and he leads his students on a day trip through the fields and forest. At the end of the hike, he serves a banquet of fresh and free foods. When he was deluged with requests for his recipes, he published his cookbook, A Few Wild Things to Eat: Gourmet Cooking with New England's Edible Wild Plants. *His recipes use everything from amaranth to yarrow. The following recipe is from Mr. Minton's book.*

* * *

Preheat the oven to 350°F.

Mix together all the ingredients, except the yogurt or sour cream. Place in a greased 5-inch by 8-inch loaf pan and bake for 17 to 20 minutes, or until heated through. Serve warm, directly from the loaf pan. Serve the yogurt or sour cream on the side.

Asparagus:
The First Treat from the Garden

The first time I saw an asparagus stalk pushing itself up from the earth, I laughed.

Until that spring I had always lived in cities. Thus, when I stumbled on fresh asparagus in my own backyard, I failed to recognize it, thinking that Edward had shoved a stalk into the ground as a joke. At the time I had just planted my first garden and was fretting over it like a new parent. "You're silly," I said as we walked to the orchard where the stalk had popped up.

"I didn't do it," he said. "And besides, I was under the impression asparagus grew in one-inch pieces cut on the diagonal."

We laughed and looked at the budding trees. The harsh New England winter was behind us. As we stood there, we felt the presence of the Lincoln family. One hundred and fifty years ago, they had hacked this clearing out of a maple, birch, and hemlock forest. The Lincolns had planted the twin crab apple trees, the rhubarb, and the sweetly perfumed lily of the valley at our feet.

The longevity of the Lincoln asparagus patch is no surprise to anyone whose family has lived for generations in one place. In Italy, for example, the present generation feasts on asparagus planted by an ancestor over two centuries ago.

Twenty-one centuries ago, Cato explained how to cultivate asparagus in his *De Re Rustica (On Farming)*. His methods are similar to those we use today. In Cato's time, the vegetable was regarded as both a pleasure and a panacea.

I don't know whether the green stalks can cure you, but I do know the arrival of the first asparagus in late February lifts my spirits more than any mood-altering drug. When the vegetable appears on the produce counter, a writer I know spends the next two weeks devising new ways to serve the delicate spears he treasures.

In French cooking, the word *Argenteuil* describes a type of asparagus, as well as a town located northwest of Paris. Argenteuil is famous for the asparagus grown there on the sandy banks of the Seine. When Impressionist artist Edouard Manet visited the town, he was inspired to paint a still life of asparagus that now hangs in the Louvre.

The English named it sparrowgrass. Diarist Samuel Pepys noted in 1667 that he purchased one hundred stalks of sparrowgrass at the Fenchurch market. When the English replaced the term sparrowgrass with asparagus, one writer protested the new word had "an air of stiffness and pedantry."

In New England, Hadley, Massachusetts, was the asparagus capital for years. Hadley is a pastoral town in the fertile Connecticut River valley where "grass," as the farmers call it, was king. But a devastating fungus disease has attacked the plant's crowns — as the roots are called — and only one hundred acres of the original one thousand still produce the crop. The town no longer hosts its gala asparagus festival.

Fusarium disease, thank goodness, hasn't affected many private plots in northern New England. Asparagus is relatively easy to grow, but you must be patient. The crowns are planted one spring and three years later, you should have an abundant harvest. It takes that long for the bed to establish itself. But once you have a thriving patch, you can count on it for at least two decades.

When planning your garden, remember to assign asparagus to the perennial section. Plant the roots on the north or east side of the patch so the fringy fronds won't shade the other plants. Unless you enjoy weeding, it is a good idea to mulch the bed to keep the competition down.

Some people make cooking asparagus a complicated matter. It needn't be. The objective is to cook the stalks without overcooking the fragile tips. Here's how: Tie the stalks in a bundle and place in a tall, slender pan. The asparagus should stand in 2 inches of boiling water. Cover and simmer for 7 to 10 minutes or until the stalks are crisp-tender. If the pan lacks a cover, use a piece of foil shaped in balloon fashion over the stalks and pinched at the edge of the pan to seal. If you have a steamer, use it to cook the vegetable.

For people who eat and cook a lot of asparagus, there is a special asparagus cooker consisting of a perforated metal sleeve that fits inside a tall, narrow pan. I have used my electric coffee percolator with good results. A victim of technology, my percolator was looking for work anyway. It had been replaced by a coffee maker programmed to brew fresh hot coffee while its owner is still befogged by sleep.

Here are some asparagus favorites to wake your taste buds to the garden's first treat.

Vinaigrette Dressing
Yield: About 1 cup

¾ cup olive oil
2 tablespoons red
  wine vinegar
1 tablespoon Dijon-
  style mustard
½ teaspoon dried
  tarragon
Salt and freshly
  ground pepper

Combine all the ingredients, adding salt and pepper to taste. Mix by whisking or shaking in a tightly sealed jar. Use to make Asparagus Beef Salad (page 70) or to dress any green salad.

Tani's Fresh Asparagus Soup
Yield: 10 to 12 servings

**2 pounds fresh
  asparagus**
Salt
Water
2 cups milk
**2 teaspoons dried
  tarragon**
**1 cup full-bodied
  white wine**
6 tablespoons butter
6 tablespoons flour
6 cups chicken stock

When Simone Beck was touring the United States, she met my colleague Tani Leach in Tulsa, Oklahoma. Tani accepted the French chef's invitation to cook and stay at her home in southern France. Tani recalls being surprised at 2 things at maison Beck: the physical labor necessary to prepare the classic French dishes and the delightful informality of the meals.

* * *

Cut the asparagus into 2-inch pieces to facilitate cooking. Boil in salted water to cover for 12 to 15 minutes until tender. Drain, then pass through a food mill to make a purée. Return to the saucepan with the milk, stirring until smooth.

Put 1 teaspoon of the tarragon into a saucepan with the wine and simmer until the liquid is reduced to about a tablespoon. Set aside.

In another saucepan, melt 4 tablespoons of the butter; stir in the flour and cook for a few seconds. Add the chicken stock, simmer a few minutes, and then add the asparagus purée.

Put a cup of the soup into the pan containing the reduced wine and tarragon. Pour through a sieve back into the pan of soup. Bring almost to a boil but do not boil. Blend the remaining 1 teaspoon tarragon with the remaining 2 tablespoons butter and stir into the soup. Serve at once.

Note: If fresh asparagus is not available, substitute 2 packages (10 ounces each) of frozen asparagus. The recipe can be cut in half if necessary.

Lois Leach's
Asparagus Casserole

Yield: 6 to 8 servings

3 cups asparagus, cut
　into 1-inch pieces
Water
6 tablespoons butter
2 tablespoons flour
2 cups milk
½ cup grated cheddar
　cheese
¼ teaspoon salt
¾ cup bread crumbs

Cook the asparagus in 1 inch of boiling water for 5 minutes. Drain and pour into a greased 9-inch square baking dish.

Melt 4 tablespoons of the butter in a heavy saucepan over medium heat. Add the flour and cook, stirring constantly until smooth and bubbly. Stir in the milk and bring to a boil, stirring constantly. Continue to stir and boil for 1 minute. Remove from the heat and add the cheese and salt. Pour over the asparagus. Top with the bread crumbs and dot with the remaining 2 tablespoons of butter. Bake in a 350°F. oven for 30 minutes. Serve hot.

Asparagus Beef Salad

Yield: 4 servings

1 pound beefsteak or
　beef roast, cooked
　medium rare
2 small onions, thinly
　sliced
1 red bell pepper, cut
　into ¼-inch strips
½ cup chopped
　walnuts
12 black olives
Vinaigrette Dressing
　(page 68)
2 pounds asparagus
Romaine lettuce
8 cherry tomatoes
Dill sprigs or Italian
　parsley

Cut the beef into 1-inch cubes. You should have 3 to 4 cups. Combine with the onions, pepper, walnuts, and olives. Toss the beef mixture with the dressing. Cover.

Peel and trim the asparagus. Boil or steam until just slightly limp. Rinse under cold water and drain carefully. Cover. Let both the beef and asparagus stand for 1 hour at room temperature.

When ready to serve, place a bed of romaine on each of 4 salad plates. Toss the asparagus with the beef and arrange on top of the romaine. Add the tomatoes. Top the asparagus with the dill or parsley and serve.

Making Peace with Rhubarb

R hubarb and I have reached an understanding. Until recently, we ignored each other. Every May, when the red stalks appeared beyond the pine grove, Edward announced, "The rhubarb is up if anyone wants to pick it."

Then he always added a description of the exciting pies of his youth.

I always responded by reciting my garden chores: the planting of the plum tomatoes, the thinning of the baby carrots, the weeding of lettuce — excitements of my youth still underway.

Before long, the rhubarb stalks produced lacy white flowers and happily went to seed. I was off the hook for another year.

Edward was not the only fan of rhubarb in my circle. Other friends offered childhood anecdotes. They spoke of sitting in the sunshine dipping the stalks in a bowl of sugar. The alternating blasts of sweet and sour kept the youngsters fascinated for most of a spring afternoon.

"It was the one time I can remember being allowed to eat sugar like that," recalled Lynn Smith, a photographer who grew up in Connecticut. "My mother was concerned about the leaves, which are poisonous. She told us to put the leaves on our heads like hats and we were just silly enough to do that."

All that sugar was one reason I rejected rhubarb. Every pie recipe seemed to call for an overdose. Any sensible person could plainly see the strawberry was the only important fruit of spring.

But coincidental gifts from friends on the same day in May changed my mind about rhubarb. First, my running partner, Cheryl Burrows, showed up one morning with a bouquet of stalks from her garden. Then Lois Leach of Westmoreland, New Hampshire, sent me a bouquet of her favorite spring recipes. Mrs. Leach has spent many of her eighty years cooking for church bazaars, town meetings, and strawberry suppers. She has taught at least three generations of the town's 4-H youngsters to bake their brownies. Although she retired several times, Mrs. Leach has kept cooking by popular demand.

One of the recipes she gave me was for a rhubarb bread she described as "really good and it camouflages the taste of the rhubarb." That's one of the mysteries of rhubarb; it is often a love/hate relationship. "My son dislikes rhubarb but loves this bread," Lois said.

I combined Cheryl's rhubarb and Lois's wisdom and made conserve, jam, crumble, and bread. Thus, rhubarb — and the thoughtfulness it inspires in New Hampshire natives — has become for me another seasonal pleasure marking the earth's journey around our star. Rhubarb has joined strawberries, parsnips, and fiddleheads in the calendar of my spirit.

The first recorded reference to rhubarb was made in 270 B.C., according to Dale E. Marshall of Michigan State University, who has compiled a 350-page bibliography on the subject. He has also planted forty-nine varieties of the fruit to test them for color, flavor, and quality. His verdict: The best varieties have a solid red petiole — as the stalk is called by botanists.

Most people plant the red-and-green Victoria variety, because it is the one freely passed around neighborhoods and down generations. It outlives people. However, if you are shopping for an all-red variety, Professor Marshall recommends Valentine or Chipman's Canada Red for color and flavor.

Rhubarb of any variety needs a cold climate because, after all, it originated in Siberia. If you garden on a porch or a patio, the plant is ideal for growing in a tub. The foliage looks cool and fresh and the flowers are attractive.

Folk medicine even prescribed a serving of rhubarb to cleanse the body. "The first rhubarb of the season is to the digestive tract of the winter-logged man what a good hot bath with plenty of healing soap is to the outer man after a bout with the plough and harrow," wrote Delia Lute in *The Country Kitchen* a half century ago. "Even the tongue and the teeth have a scrubbed feeling after a dish of early rhubarb."

How do you know when rhubarb is ripe? It's easy: Remember that the leaves are the opposite of people. When they are young, the leaves are wrinkled. When they are mature, the leaves are smooth and the stalks are ready to eat.

What can you do with rhubarb? If you have a good crop, it is a simple matter to freeze the surplus: Wash, drain well, chop, and package. In Scandinavia, the fruit is served like applesauce with pork or lamb. In England, a rhubarb-ginger jam is a favorite. In New England, the fruit is puréed and folded into whipped cream for rhubarb fool. Rhubarb wine is an easy-to-make country brew. As Edward says, "Rhubarb does whatever apples do."

Rhubarb Almond Delight
Yield: 9 servings

Crust

1 cup unbleached all-purpose flour
½ cup butter
¼ cup firmly packed brown sugar

Filling

2 eggs, beaten
¾ cup firmly packed brown sugar
¼ cup unbleached all-purpose flour
2 cups rhubarb, cut into ¼-inch pieces
½ teaspoon almond extract
½ cup slivered or coarsely chopped almonds

Here is a wonderful way to celebrate spring. This dessert is crunchy, tart, and sweet — all at once. For a special occasion, serve this dessert warm, topped with amaretto-flavored whipped cream.

* * *

Preheat the oven to 350°F.

To make the crust, combine the flour, butter, and brown sugar. Cut the ingredients together until crumbly. This can be done in a food processor. Press the mixture into a 9-inch square pan.

Mix all the filling ingredients together, except the almonds. Spoon onto the crust. Sprinkle the almonds on top. Bake for 35 to 40 minutes. Serve warm or cool.

Rhubarb Meringue Pie
Yield: 6 servings

Pie

1 tablespoon butter
4 cups rhubarb, cut into 1-inch pieces
1½ teaspoons ground cinnamon
1¼ cups sugar
2 tablespoons cornstarch
2 egg yolks, slightly beaten
¼ cup light cream
1 baked 9-inch pie shell

Meringue Topping

2 egg whites
¼ cup sugar

Preheat the oven to 350°F.

Melt the butter in a heavy skillet. Add the rhubarb, cinnamon, and 1 cup of the sugar. Cook and stir over low heat until the rhubarb is tender, about 10 minutes.

In a bowl, combine the cornstarch and remaining ¼ cup of sugar. Add the egg yolks and cream. Mix and then stir into the rhubarb mixture. Spoon the filling into the pie shell.

To make the meringue, beat the egg whites until frothy. Beat in ¼ cup sugar and continue beating until the egg whites will hold a peak. Spread the meringue over the filling, being sure to seal the meringue to the edges of the pie crust. Bake for 12 minutes, or until the meringue is a delicate brown. Cool before serving.

Note: If you are handy with a pastry tube, consider piping a meringue lattice on top of the pie. Put the meringue mixture into a pastry bag fitted with a fluted nozzle and pipe onto the pie. Bake as directed above.

Lois Leach's Rhubarb Crumble
Yield: 9 servings

Filling

4 cups rhubarb, cut into 1-inch pieces
1 tablespoon unbleached all-purpose flour
1 teaspoon grated orange rind

Topping

¾ cup unbleached all-purpose flour
¾ cup firmly packed brown sugar
Dash salt
¼ cup margarine

Preheat the oven to 350°F.

Combine the rhubarb, flour, and orange rind and place in an 8-inch square baking dish.

To make the topping, combine the flour, brown sugar, and salt. Cut in the margarine until the mixture is crumbly. Sprinkle over the rhubarb. Bake for 40 to 45 minutes. Serve warm or cooled.

Note: For a special treat, serve warm rhubarb crumble topped with whipped cream, vanilla ice cream, or flavored sour cream. To make flavored sour cream, combine ½ cup sour cream, 2 tablespoons confectioners' sugar, and ¼ teaspoon vanilla extract.

Almond Rhubarb Conserve
Yield: 5 half-pint jars

4 cups diced rhubarb
3 lemons
2 oranges
1 cup raisins
1 teaspoon almond extract
4 cups sugar
½ cup chopped almonds

A conserve is a jam gone sophisticated. The formula usually calls for a fruit in season, such as plums, grapes, or cranberries, citrus fruits, and raisins and nuts.

Conserves make wonderful gifts and can be combined with pound cake or ice cream for a spontaneous dessert. This is the first one I ever made, and it continues to be one of my favorites.

* * *

Place the rhubarb in a large, heavy kettle. Peel the lemons and oranges using a vegetable peeler. Try to get the rind off with as little of the white pith as possible. (The pith is bitter.) Finely chop the rinds and add to the rhubarb. Juice the lemons and oranges. Strain the juice and add to the kettle along with the raisins, the almond extract, the sugar, and the almonds.

Place the mixture over medium heat and stir until it comes to a boil. Lower the heat and boil gently without stirring for 45 to 60 minutes, or until the mixture is thick and clear.

My conserve generally takes about 50 minutes, but I never boil it more than 60 minutes, because the mixture gets too thick if it is cooked too long. It thickens as it cools. Pour the conserve into hot, sterilized half-pint jars, leaving ¼ inch head space, seal, and process in a boiling water bath for 5 minutes. Cool and store in a cool, dry place.

Chapter Four

Little Harvest

T he berries and peas of early summer ripen at a reasonable, almost relaxed, pace — that is, compared with the garden explosion that occurs in August. Picking and preserving the fruits of this little harvest actually can be done at leisure.

The lettuce and radishes are ready, too, but you can ignore any surplus since no one has figured out how to preserve them — except the woman who invented a recipe for lettuce bread. I choose to ignore her, too.

By this time, the peppers and beans finally look as if they are going to amount to something. But then, so do the weeds. It's up to you to decide which will win.

According to the gardener's liturgy, corn is supposed to be knee-high by the Fourth of July. My corn always sets its own schedule. Counting the hours until it's time for the fireworks down by the lake is the way the neighborhood children spend the Fourth. I delegate the sparkle of the Fourth to the fireflies. Watching them flicker and flirt around our sweet-smelling azalea bush is show enough for me.

Strawberries

A strawberry patch is a splendid place to meditate. I am reminded of this every time someone mentions how many dollars he has spent or how many continents she has crossed learning the latest method of meditation.

There is something spiritual about a clear July morning spent picking these plump, finger-staining rubies. The mind quiets down and then wanders, unhampered by its ordinary agenda.

Beyond the solitude of the row assigned to me by Farmer Richard White, I hear snatches and wisps of conversations about jams of other seasons and whether the best base for strawberry shortcake is a flaky biscuit or a sponge cake. The voices belong to the straw hats floating and bobbing above the neighboring rows.

I think about the wild strawberries that once carpeted the banks of the Piscataqua River where it separates Maine and New Hampshire. So welcome was the sight of those berries that the ocean-weary band of settlers named their new home Strawbery Banke. The year was 1630. The immigrants took advantage of the deep-running, ice-free Piscataqua and established a thriving port engaged in lumber and fishing trade. Success called for a more serious name; in the 1650s, the town was renamed Portsmouth.

Three hundred years later, most of the Strawbery Banke settlement had fallen into ruin. Much of it had been bulldozed in the name of urban renewal. But some local people became determined to save the neighborhood. Thanks to their work, we can enjoy thirty-five restored buildings located on ten acres of what now is Strawbery Banke, Inc.

I suspect the original settlers would be pleased about the new reverence for the houses they built and the cobblestone streets they walked. No doubt the prosperous merchants of that era would drink a toast to the restaurant renaissance now occurring in their neighborhood. One good restaurant after another has opened in what was once a ships' supply house or a brewery. Diners often enjoy a view of the harbor while feasting on fresh fish or lobster, followed by a strawberry dessert in season.

Strawberries combine as naturally with spirits as they do with cream. The Italians enjoy whole strawberries soaked in slightly sweetened Chianti flavored with a dash of lemon juice. Or dipped in brandy-flavored batter and deep-fried.

Other ways to spike whole, halved, or sliced berries include sprinkling with Grand Marnier, Cointreau, kirsch, or amaretto. Let the liqueur-berry mixture sit for an hour at room temperature before serving. Stir occasionally. Serve unadorned or over vanilla ice cream.

Combining the berries with champagne is a French idea. A quart of whole berries is placed in a bowl, sprinkled with sugar, and allowed to sit at room temperature. To serve, the strawberries and juice are spooned into stemmed glasses, which are then filled with a chilled dry champagne.

The French have good reason to celebrate strawberries with champagne. The strawberry as we know it today is the result of experiments done by a French botanist named Duchesne. In the eighteenth century, he successfully wed the bright red, flavorful strawberry of North America's east coast to the very large berry that grew on the west coast of South America.

An impressive way to serve whole fresh strawberries is with a bowl of melted semisweet chocolate for dipping. Or arrange them bottoms up on the surface of a cheesecake. Cover the top of the berries with a glaze made from raspberry jam that has been warmed and thinned with kirsch.

Perhaps the first strawberry shortcake was created by the native Americans when they pulverized the wild berries and stirred them into a cornmeal batter. Contemporary shortcakes may call for warm baking powder biscuits, pound cake, or sponge cake. Just avoid those bright yellow cakes sold in supermarkets by the six-pack.

Over the years, I have learned to wait until the berries are available locally. I have been disappointed by too many fool-the-eye bitter berries of late winter. When strawberries finally arrive in June, it seems like a good idea to begin a light meal with strawberry soup and end it with strawberry pie.

If I had to choose one way to eat the berries, I would opt for nibbling on them in a sun-warmed patch as I filled my tray of baskets. But I suppose one of these days a go-getter marketing strategist will advise farmers to weigh the customers before they enter the patch and again when they leave with their berries.

And then those of us who lack self-control when it comes to strawberries will pay a surcharge on our consuming passion.

Orange-Kissed Strawberries
Yield: 4 servings

1 quart strawberries
½ cup plus 1 tablespoon fine confectioners' sugar
⅓ cup Cointreau or Triple Sec
1 tablespoon kirsch
Grated rind of 1 orange
½ pint (1 cup) whipping cream
¼ cup toasted slivered almonds

Wash the berries and drain well. Hull and slice into halves. Dust the berries with ½ cup of the confectioners' sugar and add the Cointreau or Triple Sec, kirsch, and orange rind. Toss lightly. Chill in the refrigerator for no more than 2 hours or the berries will become soft.

Using a chilled small bowl and chilled beaters, beat the cream until frothy. Add the remaining 1 tablespoon confectioners' sugar and continue beating until stiff. Refrigerate. Whipped cream will maintain its consistency for about 2 hours.

Place the berries in stemmed glasses. Top with whipped cream, sprinkle with almonds, and serve.

Sophisticated Strawberries

Yield: 9 servings

1 pint strawberries
1½ cups vanilla wafer
  cookie crumbs
½ cup unsalted butter,
  melted
½ cup chopped
  pecans
½ cup firmly packed
  brown sugar
4 egg whites
½ cup plus 3
  tablespoons sugar
1 cup heavy cream

Rinse the strawberries and drain thoroughly. Preheat the oven to 350°F.

Combine the cookie crumbs, butter, pecans, and brown sugar. Press into a 9-inch square pan.

Beat the egg whites until soft peaks are formed. Gradually beat ½ cup of the white sugar into the egg whites and continue beating until stiff peaks are formed. Spoon the meringue over the crumb-pecan mixture. Bake for 16 to 17 minutes until the meringue is golden, then cool completely.

Hull and slice the berries. Sprinkle with the remaining 3 tablespoons white sugar and let stand for 15 minutes. Drain. Whip the cream and spread it over the baked meringue. Spoon on the strawberries. Chill thoroughly. Make and serve the same day.

Note: A package (10 ounces) of frozen strawberries can be substituted for the fresh berries. Thaw and drain first. Before adding sugar to the berries, taste for sweetness.

A variation of this recipe calls for placing the berries on the meringue and topping with the whipped cream. Garnish with whole berries.

Champagne Punch With Strawberries

Yield: 30 (4-ounce) servings

1 quart strawberries
½ cup sugar
Juice of 1 lemon
2 bottles (750
  milliliters each) dry
  white wine
2 bottles (750
  milliliters each)
  chilled champagne

Rinse the strawberries. Drain thoroughly and hull. Place in a punch bowl and add the sugar, lemon juice, and white wine. Chill for 3 hours. Add the champagne and serve at once.

Old-Fashioned Strawberry Shortcake

Yield: 6 servings

1 pint fresh
   strawberries
3 tablespoons sugar
2 cups unbleached all-
   purpose flour
4 teaspoons baking
   powder
½ teaspoon salt
½ cup butter
1 egg, beaten
½ cup milk
1 cup whipping cream
Melted butter

Rinse the strawberries and drain well. Hull and slice the berries, reserving a few whole berries for a garnish. Sprinkle the sliced berries with 2 tablespoons of the sugar. Set aside.

Preheat the oven to 450°F.

Sift the flour, baking powder, salt, and remaining 1 tablespoon sugar together. Cut in the butter until the mixture resembles coarse meal. Combine the egg and milk and add all at once to the flour mixture, stirring just enough to moisten.

Turn the dough out onto a lightly floured board and knead gently for 30 seconds. Pat the dough to a ½-inch thickness. Cut into 6 rounds with a floured 2½-inch cutter. Bake on an ungreased baking sheet for 10 minutes. Meanwhile, whip the cream.

While the biscuits are still warm, split and spread with the melted butter. Place berries on the bottom half of each biscuit, add the top half, and spoon whipped cream on top. Garnish with a whole berry, if desired, and serve.

Day Lilies and Snow Peas

When a chorus of orange day lilies appears at the roadside and the first snow peas ripen on the vine, I know without consulting a calendar that it is July first.

Standing in my New Hampshire garden, I feel connected somehow to the far side of the globe, where day lilies and snow peas are part of an ancient cuisine. In China, they are called *gum jum* and *ho lon dow*, respectively. I can imagine a cook in Nanjing, for example, stir-frying snow peas until they are the color of emeralds, or a gardener in Kyoto picking plump day lily buds to dip in batter and deep-fry.

In the Orient, day lily and tiger lily buds are dried, pressed into blocks, and sold by weight. The dried buds are called "golden needles"; like black mushrooms, they must be soaked before using. Shanghai chicken is a typical dish using golden needles and calls for brushing a whole chicken with soy sauce, allowing it to dry, and then deep-frying the bird for a few minutes until it is golden. The chicken is then simmered in a sauce flavored with golden needles, wood ears, and rice wine.

The day lilies in my garden generally are food for the soul rather than for the body. They make no demands on the busy gardener and thrive even in poor soil, partial shade, and drought or dampness. I like to watch as the early evening sun casts a subtle light through the blossoms. For each flower, this moment is the final show. A day lily lasts for a mere day; its genus name, *Hemerocallis,* means "beautiful for one day."

Day lily buds can be harvested when they are green or when they ripen to orange. If you cook the green, tightly closed buds they will be reminiscent of asparagus. Sauté them in hot butter for just a second or two. One fine cook serves these buds with a hollandaise sauce.

Occasionally, I harvest the plump orange buds, steam them for 3 to 5 minutes, toss with a vinaigrette dressing, and serve warm or chilled. I also try to pickle at least one jar per season. Some ambitious cooks dry their own buds, but I find it simpler to pick up a package when I visit a big city.

While I welcome the delicate white snow pea blossoms, it is the pods I hunger for. I first tasted snow peas — they were stir-fried with shrimp and flavored with oyster sauce — in a Chinese restaurant. Later, I learned the dish is Cantonese; but at the time it did not occur to me that a land as vast and diverse as China undoubtedly had several regional cuisines. Restaurants specializing in, say, Szechuan or Hunan were yet to come.

By that time, I had moved to the country. Like other refugees from Boston and New York, I learned to cook some Chinese dishes because when the urge for stir-fry strikes far from Chinatown, *you* must wield the cleaver.

When fresh snow peas appeared one spring at the produce counter, we feasted on several fine shrimp-and-snow-pea dinners — although the snow peas alone cost $2.99 a pound.

The next spring, I planted the Snowbird variety. To my amazement, the seeds sprouted and the vines flourished. I thought the Snowbird variety quite appropriate to these latitudes because the snow often flies after the peas are planted.

When the Sugar Snap variety was introduced, I switched my loyalty to it. Developed by Dr. Calvin Lamborn of Twin Falls, Idaho, for the Gallatin Seed Company, the Sugar Snaps combine the best qualities of both the snow peas and the garden variety of peas. The Sugar Snap pods are ready to pick about July first, and you can use them in any dish calling for snow peas. Wait a few days and the pods will be filled with peas. You can then eat the entire pea-filled pod, raw or cooked. That's why the French call them *mangetout* or "eat all."

The first package of Sugar Snap seeds I bought carried vague directions.

I did not train the vines upon anything and they became an impenetrable mass. Since then, I have experimented with stakes and string, chicken wire and stakes, and piles of brush. Now that I know the vines can easily reach six feet in height, I think the chicken wire arrangement is the most efficient. One gardener tells me she prefers stakes and plastic netting because they are inexpensive and easy to handle.

Whatever you do, try to eat the peas soon after picking them. Once they are picked, the peas begin to lose natural sweetness as their sugar turns to starch.

Both the Sugar Snaps and the snow peas can be briefly steamed, boiled, or stir-fried. To freeze, blanch the pods for 2 minutes in boiling water. Chill in ice water for 5 minutes. Drain thoroughly and freeze on a tray. When completely frozen, transfer to plastic bags.

I like to serve whole Sugar Snap peas with a dip at the cocktail hour. I know the edible pods filled with peas will set off conversation among my guests who are gardeners.

The passing of a platter of pickled day lily buds usually takes care of all the rest.

Rice Salad with Snow Peas

Yield: 4 to 6 servings

3 cups hot cooked rice
⅓ cup olive oil
3 tablespoons fresh lemon juice
1 pound (about 3 cups) fresh snow peas, Sugar Snaps, or shelled peas
Water
½ cup mayonnaise or plain yogurt
1 teaspoon curry powder
1 cup coarsely chopped walnuts
¼ cup chopped onion
½ cup chopped sweet red pepper
Salt and freshly ground pepper

Here is a cool, refreshing salad for a summer evening. It doubles and triples nicely for a buffet.

* * *

Combine the hot rice, olive oil, and lemon juice, mixing lightly but thoroughly. Set aside to cool.

Steam the peas over boiling water for 3 to 5 minutes, until bright green. Plunge into ice water to retain the color. Drain.

Mix the mayonnaise or yogurt with the curry powder. Set aside ¼ cup of the walnuts for a garnish. Combine the remaining ¾ cup walnuts, onion, red pepper, and curry-mayonnaise dressing with the rice. Toss lightly and season to taste with salt and pepper. Chill. Garnish with the reserved walnuts and serve.

Note: You can substitute 1 package (10 ounces) of frozen peas for the fresh. Thaw and place in boiling water for 2 minutes. Drain, plunge the peas into ice water, and drain.

Gary Fitz's Beef and Snow Peas

Yield: 4 servings

1 pound lean round or
  sirloin steak
¼ cup dry sherry
¼ cup tamari or soy
  sauce
6 tablespoons sesame
  or peanut oil
1 pound (about 3
  cups) snow peas
1 shallot, minced
½-inch piece fresh
  ginger root
1 teaspoon cornstarch
¼ cup cold water
Brown rice, egg
  noodles, or
  fettuccine
Sesame seeds, for
  garnish

Sportswriter Gary Fitz and I shared adjoining space in a crowded newsroom. With the procrastination typical of many writers, we had wonderful discussions about cooking at about 10:30 every morning. Unfortunately, 10:30 was also Gary's deadline and about once a week we received a correcting growl from sports editor Bert Rafford, a man we both admire and love.

* * *

Slice the steak thinly (¼-inch by 2-inch strips) and marinate for about 2 hours in the sherry and tamari.

Heat 3 tablespoons of the oil in a wok over high heat for about 30 seconds. Add the snow peas and stir-fry for approximately 2 minutes. Remove and keep warm in a covered bowl.

Add the remaining 3 tablespoons of the oil to the wok and heat. Add the shallot, the ginger, and the meat and marinade. Stir-fry until the meat is well browned. When the meat is almost done, stir in the pea pods.

Dissolve the cornstarch in the water and add to the wok. Stir until the sauce thickens and serve immediately with brown rice, egg noodles, or fettuccine. Garnish with sesame seeds.

Lobster Salad in Pea Pods
Yield: 50 hors d'oeuvres

50 snow or Sugar
  Snap pea pods
1 gallon boiling water
¾ cup finely chopped
  fresh, cooked
  lobster meat
½ cup finely chopped
  celery
2 tablespoons fresh
  lemon juice
¼ cup mayonnaise
⅛ teaspoon curry
  powder
Freshly ground black
  pepper

Blanch the pea pods in the boiling water for 20 seconds. Drain and immediately plunge into cold water. Drain thoroughly.

Combine the remaining ingredients, adding pepper to taste. Toss lightly.

Carefully slit open each pod along 1 seam and stuff each with a generous teaspoon of the lobster mixture. Chill.

Note: If lobster is not available, substitute chicken or turkey.

Snow Pea and Mushroom Salad
Yield: 6 servings

1 pound (about 3
  cups) snow peas or
  Sugar Snaps
Water
2 cups fresh
  mushrooms
½ cup fresh lemon
  juice
1 cup olive oil
2 tablespoons soy
  sauce
1 tablespoon sugar
¼ cup sesame seeds
Freshly ground black
  pepper

This salad goes nicely with chicken and pork.

* * *

Steam the snow peas over boiling water for 5 minutes. Rinse with cold water to retain the bright color. Drain. Slice the mushrooms and toss with the snow peas.

Mix the remaining ingredients, except the black pepper. Whisk or stir until the sugar is dissolved. Toss with the snow peas and mushrooms. Add pepper to taste. Chill for several hours or serve immediately.

Note: Fresh green beans, cut into 1-inch lengths, can be substituted for the snow peas or Sugar Snaps.

Lauren's
Chicken with Lily Buds

Yield: 4 servings

3-pound chicken, cut into serving pieces
¼ cup plus 1 tablespoon soy sauce
1 cup dried day lily buds
1 teaspoon sugar
2 teaspoons dry sherry
4 cups chicken broth or bouillon
Freshly ground black pepper
2 tablespoons oil
2 garlic cloves, minced
½ cup chopped onion
1-inch piece fresh ginger root, minced
1 tablespoon cornstarch
3 tablespoons cold water
1 tablespoon sesame seeds, for garnish

Place the chicken on a cake rack. Brush the chicken with ¼ cup soy sauce. Let it dry for about 30 minutes.

Place the lily buds in a bowl and cover with hot water. Let them soak for 20 minutes. Drain and set aside.

Mix the remaining 1 tablespoon soy sauce, sugar, sherry, chicken broth or bouillon, and 3 grinds of black pepper. Set aside.

Heat the oil in a large, heavy frying pan. Brown the chicken on all sides over medium heat; this should take about 10 minutes. Remove the chicken from the pan. Place the garlic, onion, and ginger root in the pan and cook for 1 minute. Slowly add the broth to the pan. Then add the chicken and day lily buds. Bring to a boil and simmer, covered, for 25 minutes. Remove the chicken to a platter.

Dissolve the cornstarch in the cold water and add to the pan. Cook and stir for a few minutes until the sauce thickens slightly. Pour the sauce over the chicken, garnish with sesame seeds, and serve.

Note: A cup of sliced, sautéed mushrooms can be substituted for the day lily buds.

Salmon and Peas
For the Fourth of July

The first time I heard someone say she was serving salmon and peas for a Fourth of July dinner party, I nearly choked on a mouthful of tomato aspic.

The scene was a ladies' luncheon — an intimate but fast-disappearing rite of sisterhood. A kindly grand dame had invited me to lunch with her colleagues on the board of some worthy institution. She served her guests a variety of molded salads on a table decorated with pink napery and lavender lilacs. For me, it was a pleasant break from ordinary working lunches, which too often consist of unmemorable food at an overpriced theme restaurant or a cup of yogurt and a few carrot sticks eaten in the flickering glare of a computer terminal.

In any case, the woman who was carrying on about the salmon and peas was a pretentious person, and as she elaborated on her upcoming menu, I grew even more confused.

All I knew about that combination was a dish called Salmon Wiggle. It appeared in a 1940 Girl Scout cookbook and the ingredients — presumably for camping convenience — all came out of cans: a can each of peas, salmon, and evaporated milk. The name was the most interesting thing about the dish. Girl Scouts in my neighborhood cooked this bland, gummy stuff in the church basement after spending the Fourth of July morning burning tattered American flags. It was a two-badge event: one for dispatching the flags, one for making a camper's lunch.

All of that passed through my mind as I ate the aspic, and by the time Mrs. Pretentious got to the part about a poacher large enough to hold twenty-five servings of fish, I realized that we were not thinking about the same dish at all.

A few years later, some people were celebrating the Fourth by sitting and rocking on the front porch of a boarding house in town. How, someone asked, did the salmon and pea tradition get started? The landlady was elected to call me at the newspaper. I told her I would find the answer sometime before the next meeting of the Fourth of July front-porch forum.

"It was a matter of pride with my grandfather," explained a thirty-year-old Yankee friend. "He took great pleasure in having his peas and new potatoes ready by the Fourth."

But some of the boarders were as old as my friend's grandfather and they recalled *their* grandparents serving the menu. I sought the answer through a newspaper classified ad.

A New Hampshire native wrote from Florida, "Abigail Adams is one of my favorite historical figures, much admired, so please include her menu. She served salmon with egg sauce at her Fourth of July dinner parties." Abigail's menu also included apple pandowdy and turtle soup. My Florida correspondent added, "My great-grandpa used to catch a turtle, put it in a barrel, fatten the creature, and eventually make a fine soup."

More than one writer pointed out the tradition went beyond New Hampshire. "My husband and I were both brought up on the north shore of Boston, and our families always had salmon and peas for the Fourth. Ideally, the salmon was poached and served with a creamed egg sauce. The peas were the first new peas and were usually planted on April 19, Patriots' Day. I can remember going to my grandmother's for this holiday meal. The dessert was ice cream with strawberry sauce. And there were party favors that resembled red, white, and blue packages of firecrackers. When you unwrapped them, you found a peppermint stick."

Another writer said her ancestors in both Maine and Nova Scotia observed the salmon-and-peas ritual. "One of my earliest memories is the adults checking their peas to see if they would be ready for the Fourth. As a child, I nearly believed that one of the Ten Commandments was, 'Thou shalt eat peas and salmon on the Fourth of July.' "

In colonial times, the Connecticut River ran thick with Atlantic salmon swimming up river to spawn. By 1814, dams built by the settlers led to the extinction of the river salmon. Thanks to the efforts of environmentalists, the government and utility companies with dams on the river are spending millions of dollars building fish ladders to bring the salmon back to the upper Connecticut River.

Perhaps there will come a day when salmon becomes as ordinary as chicken. Like the times alluded to in *A History of Walpole, New Hampshire:* "Salmon was so common that Colonel Benjamin Bellows' hired men stipulated they would not have it oftener than three times a week."

Cape Cod Salmon Steaks
Yield: 4 servings

4 salmon steaks, each
  1 inch thick
½ cup dry white
  vermouth
Juice of ½ lemon
1 cup sour cream, at
  room temperature
½ cup chopped green
  onions
2 tablespoons Dijon-
  style mustard
Salt and freshly
  ground pepper
Dill sprigs, for
  garnish

A house guest from New York City introduced me to this simple but festive dish. When I asked for the recipe, she said, "It's not mine. I got it from an inn on Cape Cod." Well, the recipe is back in New England, and I have discovered it adapts nicely to other fish, other seasonings, and yogurt in place of the sour cream.

* * *

Marinate the salmon in the vermouth and lemon juice in a nonmetallic bowl for 2 hours before cooking.

Mix the remaining ingredients, except the dill, adding salt and pepper to taste. When you are ready to cook, remove the salmon from the marinade with a slotted spoon and place in an aluminum-foil-lined shallow baking dish. Broil 6 inches from the heat for 7 minutes. Turn the steaks over and spread with the sour cream mixture. Broil for 5 minutes, or until lightly browned. Be careful not to overcook. Garnish with dill and serve at once.

Poached Salmon With Egg Sauce

Yield: 8 servings

5-pound to 7-pound
  salmon, cleaned
1 lemon, thinly sliced
3 tablespoons butter
3 tablespoons flour
2 cups milk
½ teaspoon salt
½ teaspoon ground
  cloves
2 tablespoons
  chopped parsley
2 hard-cooked eggs,
  coarsely chopped

Abigail Adams is said to have started the custom of serving poached salmon with egg sauce on the Fourth of July. You may serve the warm salmon on a platter decorated with watercress, sorrel, or parsley and lemon slices. Pass the egg sauce separately in a warmed sauce boat. Complete the menu with steamed fresh peas.

The poached salmon can be served chilled. In that case, serve it with homemade herbed mayonnaise. To each cup of mayonnaise, add ½ cup of assorted finely chopped fresh herbs. Such a combination might include watercress, parsley, chervil, chives, and tarragon.

* * *

Preheat the oven to 450°F.

Rinse the fish and pat dry. Place some of the lemon slices in the cavity. Place the fish on a large piece of heavy-duty aluminum foil. Top the fish with the remaining lemon slices. Wrap the fish in the foil and secure the ends so the juices won't escape. Place the package in an oblong baking pan and bake for 45 minutes, or until the fish flakes easily. Do not overcook. Serve the salmon warm with the egg sauce on the side.

To make the sauce, melt the butter in a saucepan over medium heat. Add the flour and cook, stirring, until the mixture bubbles, about 2 minutes. Slowly stir in the milk and continue cooking and stirring until the sauce thickens and boils. Let it boil for 1 minute. Add the remaining ingredients and heat through. Serve at once.

Note: If you want to remove the skin from the fish before serving, do so carefully with a sharp knife. Don't mar the smooth flesh beneath the skin if you can manage.

Smoked Salmon Spread

Yield: 1½ cups

8 ounces cream cheese, cut into chunks
¼ pound smoked salmon
Juice of ½ lemon
Dash Tabasco sauce
1 tablespoon fresh dill weed
Dark rye rounds

Using a food processor fitted with a steel blade, process the cream cheese until softened and smooth. Add the salmon and process until thoroughly mixed. Add the seasonings and process only until mixed. Serve with rye rounds as an appetizer.

Blueberries for Slumps, Grunts, and Buckles

When I spread a bit of blueberry jam on my breakfast toast, I feel like Scottish royalty.

Blueberry jam, the story goes, was invented in the court of James V. His French wife, Madeleine, brought her own cooks when she moved into the castle in Scotland. The cooks harvested the local wild berries for a jam to wake up the court's tired palates. That jam was actually called "blae berry" jam — "blae" being the Scottish word for blue black.

When we North Americans claim the blueberry for a native, we are only half wrong. The cultivated blueberry is indeed an American native. But the wild, scrubby, low-bush blueberry grew all over Europe and Asia. Russian women, for example, used the berry for food and to cure stomachaches. On this side of the Atlantic, Indians dried the berry and used it during the winter months as they would currants or raisins.

Blueberry cultivation began in the United States just after the turn of the century. Elizabeth White, a New Jersey woman, is undoubtedly the mother of the commercial blueberry. She donated acres and acres and a good deal of time to cultivation experiments, concluding that blueberries only grow in acid soil. Blueberries belong to the heath family. Other family members — mountain laurel, rhododendron, and azalea — also thrive in our New England acid soil.

Blueberries — cultivated and wild — flourish over much of the North

American continent. They are harvested from the Canadian Maritime provinces to as far south as Florida. Blueberries are grown to the west in Michigan and along the West Coast from northern California to Alaska.

North Americans consume 105 million pounds of the frosty blues annually. New Jersey and Michigan are the leaders in the cultivated-crop production. Maine leads the states in the wild blueberry harvest and Nova Scotia (New Scotland) appropriately leads the provinces.

Unlike in Scotland, the eating of blueberries was not an uppercrust preserve in colonial North America. In fact, in early America, the eating of blueberries seems more closely related to humble pie. The names of the blueberry dishes favored in New England reflect their folksy origins: blueberry grunt, blueberry roly-poly, blueberry slump, blueberry flummery, and blueberry buckle.

When I first moved to New Hampshire, I discovered an abundance of both high-bush and low-bush berries in our dooryard. All for free. I made nearly everything — from blueberry soup to blueberry pie.

I canned all the rest simply because the blueberries in the muffin mixes packed by Betty Crocker came in little cans. And if canning was good enough for Betty . . .

Then I learned how to make jam, which was simpler than canning berries. These days, I freeze the berries in shallow baking pans. When the berries are frozen, I pour them into quart containers. Come January, I just pour out what I need for a quick bread or pancakes.

Blueberries, of course, are not everyone's favorite berry.

Food authority James Beard wrote that given a choice, he would rather eat strawberries or raspberries. He did concede, however, "I can definitely recommend a combination of blueberries with maple syrup and cream or blueberries with peaches and maple syrup."

Slumps, grunts, and buckles are the traditional ways to deal with blueberries in my corner of New Hampshire. How do you tell a slump from a grunt?

One New Hampshire native tells me both slumps and grunts call for biscuit dough. But slumps are baked and grunts are steamed. The biscuit dough slumps into the fruit as it bakes and grunt is the sound of the dumplings steaming.

Buckles, she says, are cakes with a baked-on crumb topping of butter, cinnamon, and flour. These cakes may or may not collapse or buckle during baking. If any cake falls during baking, an enterprising cook may want to bring it to the table under the title Blueberry (or whatever) Buckle.

The Melt-in-Your-Mouth Blueberry Cake is a popular New Hampshire cake. Leona Fisk of Charlestown, New Hampshire, was the first to give me the recipe. Her son Carlton, a catcher for the Chicago White Sox, ate his share of this cake as a boy. You won't need this item to sell the cake to your diners, but you never know when you might need to patch up a lull in a dinner conversation with a baseball fact.

Melt-in-Your-Mouth
Blueberry Cake

Yield: 8 servings

2 eggs, separated
1½ cups blueberries
1½ cups sifted
    unbleached all-
    purpose flour
1 teaspoon baking
    powder
½ cup margarine
1 cup sugar
⅓ cup milk
1 teaspoon vanilla
    extract
Cream sherry
    (optional)

Preheat the oven to 350°F.

Beat the egg whites until stiff. In a separate bowl, beat the yolks. Toss the berries with a little flour and set aside. Sift the remaining flour and baking powder 3 times.

Cream the margarine and sugar and add the well-beaten egg yolks.

Add the milk and flour mixture alternately to the creamed mixture. Fold in the beaten egg whites and vanilla. Add the blueberries. Turn into a greased 8-inch square baking pan.

Bake for 35 to 45 minutes, or until a tester inserted in the middle of the cake comes out clean.

Serve warm as a pudding, laced with a bit of cream sherry. Or serve cooled as a cake.

Blueberry Grunt

Yield: 4 to 5 servings

2 cups blueberries
½ cup sugar
1 cup water
1 cup unbleached all-
    purpose flour
2 teaspoons baking
    powder
½ cup milk
Plain or whipped
    cream

Mix the blueberries, sugar, and water in a saucepan. Bring to a boil and cook over low heat for about 10 minutes.

Stir the flour and baking powder together; add the milk and stir just enough to mix. Drop by the tablespoon over the berries. Cover tightly and cook for 15 minutes. During the cooking, keep the heat just high enough to keep the berries bubbling.

Serve warm with plain or whipped cream.

Orange-Blueberry Bread
Yield: 1 loaf

1 cup blueberries
2 cups sifted
    unbleached all-
    purpose flour
½ cup sugar
1½ teaspoons baking
    powder
½ teaspoon salt
½ teaspoon baking
    soda
½ cup chopped
    walnuts
1 teaspoon grated
    orange rind
1 egg
¾ cup orange juice
2 tablespoons
    vegetable oil

Preheat the oven to 350°F.

Sprinkle the blueberries with a bit of the flour and toss lightly. Sift together the remaining flour, sugar, baking powder, salt, and baking soda. Stir in the blueberries, nuts, and orange rind. Set aside.

Combine the egg, orange juice, and oil. Add to the flour-fruit mixture. Stir just until moistened.

Pour into a greased 5-inch by 9-inch loaf pan. Bake for 50 minutes, or until lightly browned.

Place the pan on a rack and cool for 10 minutes. Carefully run a sharp knife around the edges of the pan, invert, and remove the loaf from the pan. Cool on the rack.

Blueberry Jam
Yield: Approximately 12 half-pint jars

1 lemon
1½ quarts blueberries
7 cups sugar
1 bottle (6 ounces)
    liquid fruit pectin

Grate the rind of the lemon. Squeeze out the juice. Crush the blueberries in a kettle. Add the lemon juice and rind. Add the sugar and mix well. Place over high heat and bring to a rolling boil. Boil for 1 minute, stirring constantly.

Remove from the heat. All at once, stir in the pectin. Stir and skim off any foam for about 5 minutes.

Ladle into hot, sterilized half-pint jars, leaving ¼ inch head space. Seal. Process in a boiling water bath for 5 minutes. Cool and store in a cool, dry place.

Chapter Five

Haying

I needed to buy a wood stove, but the dealer already had a date for every night in July. He was haying, and the crop wouldn't wait. Haying is one of the hottest, stickiest, prickliest jobs there is. But when the work is done, even the passersby are rewarded with the clean, sweet smell of a freshly mowed field.

In this season, keeping cool seems to be one's life's work. A breeze is a major event. Going to a good movie used to be a way to beat the heat for a few hours. But then someone decided there should be movies made just for summer and that they all had to be awful. Thank goodness we can still escape to the cool, green depths of the pine forest.

Talk about dog days. Our ordinarily dignified cat looks quite foolish during this hot spell. After washing herself, China doesn't have the energy to pull her tongue back in; it just hangs there looking dumb.

When the humidity hangs on, cold soups and chilled salads are just right for dinner. Then, suddenly, the beans must be picked. It's time to preserve the dilly beans for winter. Did I say haying was the hottest work?

Water and Other Summer Coolers

When the weather forecast becomes a three-word alliteration — hot, hazy, and humid — I am reminded of my friend Francis. He lives in a nearby town where the people drink what they call "city water," which is piped into their houses from a pond in the hills.

According to Francis, city water produces cloudy ice cubes, whereas the water from our well freezes into polished diamonds. Each summer, he appears on a day when the heat rises off the earth in great waves. He carries a bouquet of mint or a clump of iris tubers thinned from his garden and a couple of empty jugs. Francis was importing country water long before it became fashionable to buy the bottled kind with French names and fancy labels.

Edward and I are blessed with an abundant supply of potable water. We need no gadgets that dispense chilled water from the refrigerator door or automatically crank out more ice cubes in one day than we could use in a season. Our water is pumped from deep inside the earth where nature keeps it cold and fresh.

But we have neighbors who are less fortunate. One family struck a plentiful source only to discover it contained large amounts of iron that dye the laundry orange and coat just-shampooed hair with a nasty residue. Other neighbors never achieved a year-round source of running water. Despite deep and expensive drilling, they only hit a ledge of granite.

When we first moved to the country, a shallow well supplied our water. By August every year, the well ran dry until it was replenished by the rains of autumn. During the drought months, we lugged cans of drinking water and bathed discreetly in a nearby lake.

We eventually gambled on drilling an artesian well. Each evening, hours after the digger had quit for the day, the thud-thud-thud of his machinery echoed in our heads. But the pounding paid off. Within days, our man had struck an underground lake, the source of more gallons-per-minute than we had ever hoped for.

Seasonal drought, it turns out, is a minor inconvenience. We now know there are worse things that can happen to our water, including poisoning by road salt, pesticides, toxic waste, acid rain, and thermonuclear pollution. And I am talking about the threats to the water in just one New England valley.

Thus, even in these days of water wealth in our house and garden, Edward and I still conserve this precious liquid. We can remember the times we turned on the faucet to wash our hands and nothing happened.

The Lincoln family, who built our house and farmed the surrounding fields, grew hay among other crops. Haying is brutal labor that must be done during the hottest weather of the year. The Lincolns probably guzzled switchel as they cut, raked, and bundled hay.

Switchel, also known as haymakers' tea, contains molasses, water, vinegar, and ginger. Vinegar is a main ingredient in another traditional Yankee cooler, raspberry shrub, which consists of the fruit juice, vinegar, and sugar or honey. Perhaps the acid in vinegar — like the acid in lemonade — is what slakes the thirst.

As electric rates climb, I take satisfaction in making sun tea, which requires no special equipment despite what you read in mail-order gadget catalogs. All you do is place 3 to 4 tablespoons of black or herbal tea leaves in a half-gallon bottle and fill it with cold water. Place in the sun before noon. By three o'clock, the brew will be steeped and ready to strain and chill. No harm will be done if you have to let the tea steep a few hours longer.

Concord grape juice is also simple to make. My friend Olin brings me a bushel of these wild native American grapes every autumn. I put up two dozen quarts of juice and let it ripen over the winter. All it costs is a couple hours and the price of six cups of honey. This light red juice can be frozen into refreshing pops, which young mothers tell me delight their toddlers but do not dye the fronts of little shirts a deep purple.

In the old days, New Englanders who drank spirits cooled off with rum-laced lemonade or a "stone fence," which was made of cold apple cider with a shot of rum.

Some contemporary summer drinks include the New England cooler, a combination of cranberry juice and rum; sangria, based on dry red wine and fruit juice; and the mimosa, a wedding reception favorite made of champagne and orange juice.

If you object to the overpriced beverages sold at airport snack bars or the insolent service at interstate highway restaurants, you'll enjoy the spirit of Dr. A. W. Chase's portable lemonade. His recipe for Pocket Lemonade appeared in his 1866 edition of *Practical Recipes.* Dr. Chase's formula called for mixing one pound of pulverized sugar with one-half ounce each of citric acid and lemon essence. A wise traveler always carried a teaspoon of the mixture wrapped in paper, and when overcome by thirst added the pocket lemonade to a cup of spring water.

"All the beauties of lemonade will be there waiting to be drunk without costing a penny," the thrifty doctor noted.

Switchel or Haymakers' Tea

Yield: About 20 (8-ounce) servings

1 gallon water
2 cups sugar
1 cup molasses
1 cup cider vinegar or
hard cider
1 teaspoon ground
ginger

The year was 1908. Gladys Johnson was 10 years old and living on her parents' farm in Stoddard, New Hampshire. "At that time, money was scarce and farmers used to trade work," she recalls. "At haying time, mother used to make this drink for the men and serve it ice cold from earthenware jugs. She claimed they could drink it and not get any ill effects from the heat. My grandmother was part Indian, and I think it might have been something she used to make. She always had a remedy for our ills hanging from the rafters in the attic."

* * *

Mix well and serve chilled.

Charley's Fish House Punch

Yield: 12 to 15 servings

6 lemons
2 cups firmly packed
light brown sugar
6 cups water
1 bottle (750
milliliters) dark
rum
½ bottle (375
milliliters) cognac
½ cup peach brandy
1 ice ring

Juice the lemons and place the juice and rinds in a bowl.

Mix the brown sugar and water and boil gently for 5 minutes. Pour into the bowl with the lemons and cool.

Strain the lemon juice-sugar mixture and pour into a large crock. Add the rum and brandies. Stir gently and taste. Add more peach brandy, if desired.

Cover the crock and let the punch sit overnight before serving. To serve, place an ice ring in a punch bowl and pour the punch over.

Note: To make an ice ring, pour 5½ cups of water or pineapple juice in a 1½-quart ring mold and freeze for 6 hours or overnight.

Bloody Basil

Yield: 4 servings

2 quarts very ripe
  tomatoes
¼ cup sugar
½ cup fresh basil
  leaves
¼ cup rum

Here is a refreshing way to start a meal on a summer day. For gardeners, it's one solution to the August tomato explosion.

* * *

Cut the tomatoes into chunks, bring to a boil, and cook gently for 30 minutes. Put the tomatoes through a sieve or food mill to remove the skins and seeds. Stir in the sugar. Let the juice stand until water rises to the top, about 1 hour. Scoop off the excess water. You should have about 1 quart of liquid left.

Combine half of the juice and half of the basil in a blender. Blend until the basil is finely chopped. Repeat. Stir in the rum and chill. Serve cold.

Note: You can substitute 1 quart prepared juice for the fresh tomatoes.

Cape Cod
Cranberry Cooler

Yield: 6 (4-ounce) servings

4 cups fresh or frozen
  cranberries
1½ cups orange juice
½ cup Burgundy
1 cup sugar
1 teaspoon grated
  orange rind

Mix all the ingredients in a large saucepan and cook until the berries pop, about 5 minutes. Strain the mixture through a sieve, pushing the pulp and juice through with the back of a spoon. Discard any pulp remaining in the sieve. Cool.

Pour the cranberry mixture into a shallow pan. Cover and freeze until firm, 1 to 3 hours. Thaw slightly and break the mixture into chunks. Place half of the mixture into a food processor bowl fitted with a metal blade. Whirl until the mixture is slushy but not thawed. Pour into chilled glasses. Repeat. Serve with spoons.

Note: If you don't have cranberries, substitute 4 cups of cranberry cocktail, decreasing the sugar to taste.

Great-Aunt Minnie's Old-Fashioned Lemonade

Yield: About 8 (8-ounce) servings

2 large lemons
½ to ¾ cup sugar
½ gallon water
Thinly sliced lemon, fresh mint, or strawberry or cherry, for garnish

Roll the lemons on a hard surface to soften them for extracting more juice. Peel with a swivel-bladed peeler and reserve the rind. Squeeze the lemons and strain the juice.

Combine the sugar, water, rind, and juice. Stir vigorously and chill. Serve with ice and garnish with a fresh slice of lemon, a sprig of mint, or a fresh strawberry or cherry.

Fresh Raspberry Ice Cream Soda

Yield: 6 servings

½ gallon very good vanilla ice cream
2 cups fresh raspberries
1 bottle (750 milliliters) champagne

Fill 6 tall soda glasses two-thirds full with alternating layers of ice cream and raspberries. Fill the glasses to the top with champagne and serve.

Note: For a nonalcoholic ice cream soda, substitute ginger ale or club soda for the champagne. Sodas may be varied by using other fruits of summer, such as strawberries, peaches, nectarines, or cantaloupe.

Rhubarb Cooler

Yield: 10 servings (3½ quarts)

4 cups rhubarb, sliced into ½-inch pieces
½ cup sugar
4 cups water
¾ cup orange juice
½ cup fresh lemon juice
2 quarts chilled ginger ale
Mint sprigs, for garnish

Combine the rhubarb, sugar, and water and cook over low heat until the rhubarb is mushy, about 20 minutes. Purée in a blender. Add additional water if needed to make 4 cups. Add the orange juice and lemon juice and chill.

Before serving, stir in the ginger ale. Garnish with mint sprigs.

Sangria

¼ to ½ cup Simple
Syrup (recipe under
Note)
1 bottle (750
milliliters) dry red
wine
½ cup brandy
1 cup orange juice
2 tablespoons lemon
juice
1 cup chilled club
soda
1 lemon, thinly sliced
1 orange, thinly sliced
1 lime, thinly sliced

Mix the Simple Syrup, wine, brandy, and fruit juices in a large pitcher. Chill.

Just before serving, add the club soda. Serve over ice in tall glasses or large wine glasses. Add a slice of each fruit to each glass.

Note: Simple Syrup is used to sweeten cold drinks, such as iced tea or coffee. The Simple Syrup dissolves readily, whereas sugar usually settles undissolved at the bottom of the glass. To make the syrup, simmer together 1 cup water and 1 cup sugar for 5 to 10 minutes, or until clear. Cool. Store in a tightly covered jar, but do not refrigerate. Makes 1½ cups.

Easy Concord Grape Juice

Concord grapes
Honey
Boiling water

Wash and stem the grapes. Place 1 cup of grapes into each hot, sterilized quart canning jar. Add ¼ cup of honey to each jar and fill to ½ inch of the rim with boiling water. Seal the jars and process for 10 minutes in a boiling water bath. Cool and store in a cool, dry place.

Let the flavor develop for at least 2 weeks before serving.

Note: Honey will be easier to pour if it is slightly warmed.

The Politics of Zucchini

You can laugh all you want at the vegetable zucchini but the slim, green cucurbit has launched at least one political career.

I am not talking about the patronizing buffoonery displayed by politicians gobbling a burrito or a pastrami sandwich in neighborhoods where they need votes. Instead, this political career began in a picture-postcard town where some parents needed to raise money for their children's school.

Taking advantage of the predictable zucchini surplus afflicting every gardener around, the parents invented the International Zucchini Festival. The activities included a zucchini look-alike contest, a parade of zukes, a zucchini relay race, and a zucchini peeling competition. By sunset on that silly day in August, the school was several thousand dollars ahead, and the zucchini doings had been filmed for the rest of America via NBC's "Real People."

Several zucchini festivals later, one of the founding mothers decided to apply that kind of energy to politics and after winning a minor state office she was off and running for a major one.

Gardeners, it turns out, visit newspaper offices as frequently as politicians. Every spring, at least one person races to the newsroom where I work to report picking the first pea of the season. Then come the gardeners bearing two-headed radishes, six-pronged carrots, giant pumpkins, and eggplants that resemble unpopular politicians.

However, when someone brings in a monster zucchini and smiles proudly for the camera, I cannot join in the way-to-go-fella back slapping. I know — as does any gardener — that it's foolish to allow a zucchini to become a baseball bat. It's the mark of a novice, of someone who could not stay on top of things and who let this giant slurp the water and nutrients needed by the cabbages and carrots.

I do understand how it happens. When the first zucchini of the season reaches six inches in length, you steam and stir-fry with a certain reverence. Then you make ratatouille and frittata. Of course, you can't freeze or can zucchini for the winter because it gets soggy and tastes terrible. You stop harvesting the vegetable and hope the rabbits or raccoons will take charge.

Instead, the zucchini get revenge and grow out of control. They become tough, unpalatable, and full of seeds. There are those who try to redeem their harvest at this point by shredding the monsters and making chocolate cakes. All in the name of frugality. I suspect the sugar-laden zucchini bundt cakes are just one more excuse to calorify. Do yourself a favor and toss these useless clubs onto the compost heap.

Now, if you don't know your squashes, here's a quick course. Squash, pumpkins, melons, and cucumbers are members of the cucurbit family. Like some human families, the cucurbits grow curls or tendrils and take up a lot of space as they grow and mature.

The squash branch of the family is conveniently divided into two seasons. Winter squash, like the season, lasts a long time. Butternut, acorn, and Hubbard are the most popular winter squashes. They can be prepared like a pumpkin: baked, stuffed, steamed, boiled, or made into a pie.

Gourds and spaghetti squash are also members of the winter branch. Vegetable spaghetti will keep for several months if stored in a cool place; where you keep the pumpkin and acorn squash will be just right.

The summer branch of the cucurbit family resembles the season: fleeting and most enjoyable when young. Some traditional summer squashes include the green zucchini, golden zucchini, yellow crookneck, and patty pan, also know as a white scallop squash. A new hybrid, called Globe zucchini, looks like a deep green tennis ball.

Summer squash can be eaten raw like a cucumber. I like to surround a bowl of hummus or other dip with fingers of alternating green and gold zucchini.

Only the zucchini has captured the attention of cookbook authors who have written entire works on this single vegetable. Their recipes include zucchini raisin pie, zucchini shaslik, ragout of summer squash, and zucchini spice cake. As far as I know, the only omissions are zucchini daiquiris and zucchini liqueur.

There is even a European zucchini diet that is said to cleanse the skin and lighten the body. You eat nothing but steamed lemon-flavored zucchini for three days. You may have water and some fruit juice. As with all single-food diets, you might lose a few pounds, but you will certainly lose any fondness for the vegetable.

If you want to nip the zucchini profusion in the bud, consider stuffing the blossoms with a bit of mozzarella and an anchovy, dipping them in batter, and deep-frying until golden.

Until recently, I thought zucchini was immune to the special-equipment mystique. Then I read about a zucchini corer offered by one of those fancy California mail-order catalogs. You use it to stuff a zucchini with rice and ground lamb. The rosewood handle should keep your spirits up while you core away the afternoon.

Rolled Stuffed Fish Fillets

Yield: 4 servings

2 tablespoons olive oil
1 medium-size (12 ounces) zucchini, cut into 5-inch sticks
¼ teaspoon fresh dill weed
4 fish fillets (total weight about 1 pound)
3 tablespoons melted butter
2 tablespoons lemon juice
½ cup grated cheddar cheese
Paprika
Chopped fresh parsley

Preheat the oven to 350°F.

Heat the olive oil and sauté the zucchini until just crisp-tender. Add the dill weed and toss lightly.

Place ¼ of the zucchini on the narrow end of each of the 4 fillets. Beginning at the narrow end, roll up and secure with toothpicks. Place the fish, seam side down, in a greased baking dish. Drizzle with butter and lemon juice. Bake for 15 minutes. Top with the cheese and sprinkle with paprika and parsley. Bake for 10 minutes more, or until the fish flakes easily when tested with a fork. Remove the picks before serving.

Note: I use cod or haddock but you can use any firm-fleshed white meat fillets.

Zucchini Bread

Yield: 2 loaves

3 eggs
2 cups sugar
1 cup oil
1 teaspoon vanilla
  extract
2 cups grated raw
  zucchini
3 cups unbleached all-
  purpose flour
1 teaspoon baking
  soda
¼ teaspoon baking
  powder
1 teaspoon salt
1 tablespoon ground
  cinnamon
1 teaspoon ground
  cloves
1 cup chopped
  walnuts
1 teaspoon grated
  orange rind

Preheat the oven to 350°F. Grease two 4½-inch by 8½-inch loaf pans.

Beat the eggs, sugar, oil, and vanilla. Fold in the grated zucchini.

Sift the dry ingredients together. Stir into the zucchini mixture until just blended. Fold in the nuts and orange rind. Pour the batter into the prepared pans.

Bake for 1 hour, or until a cake tester inserted in the center comes out clean. Cool for 10 minutes and remove from the pans. Cool completely on racks. For best flavor, wrap the breads when cool and let them stand overnight before serving.

Herb Bouquet Zucchini Soup

Yield: 6 servings

1 pound (3 to 4 small)
  zucchini, sliced
1 cup chicken stock
Sea salt
¼ teaspoon dried
  basil
¼ teaspoon dried
  thyme
¼ teaspoon dried
  marjoram
2 cups milk
Yogurt (optional)

Combine the zucchini, stock, and salt to taste in a saucepan and bring to a boil. Cover and simmer gently until tender, about 20 minutes. Cool.

Add the herbs. Purée the soup in a blender. Add the milk and heat, but do not boil. Serve with a dab of yogurt, if desired.

This soup also can be served chilled.

Ratatouille

Yield: 12 servings

½ cup olive oil
1 cup coarsely
  chopped onion
4 garlic cloves,
  minced
2 medium-size
  eggplants, cut into
  1-inch cubes
6 to 8 small zucchini,
  cut into ¼-inch
  slices
2 green peppers,
  seeded and chopped
2 sweet red peppers,
  seeded and chopped
4 medium-size
  tomatoes, peeled
  and chopped
1 tablespoon dried
  oregano
1 tablespoon dried
  basil
½ teaspoon dried
  thyme
Salt
Freshly ground
  pepper

Making ratatouille is one way to cope with an exploding garden. It combines all the flavors of late summer and can be enjoyed hot, warm, or cold. The friend who gave me this recipe suggests making it in an electric frying pan, but I prefer a Dutch oven.

* * *

In a Dutch oven, heat ¼ cup of the olive oil. Add the onion and garlic and sauté until soft. Add the remaining ¼ cup oil, the eggplants, and zucchini and sauté for 5 minutes.

Add the peppers, tomatoes, and herbs. Cover and simmer for 30 minutes. Remove the cover and simmer for 10 minutes to allow some of the liquid to evaporate. Add salt and pepper to taste.

Note: Use fresh herbs if available: 4 chopped basil leaves, 10 chopped oregano leaves, and a pinch of thyme.

Eggplant:
From Raging Apple to Aphrodisiac

I fell in love with the color of the eggplant long before I learned to appreciate its versatile flesh. If I were naming a Crayola® after the vegetable, I would call it Midnight Purple.

One year I planted an eggplant seedling because I lusted for touches of that royal color among the green rows of the August garden.

My total crop was one eggplant. Since then I have learned the vegetable thrives in sandy soil that is characteristic of southern New Jersey. Now I delegate my eggplant impulses to the Garden State farmers who take the matter quite seriously. In fact, in Vineland, New Jersey, the annual eggplant festival is topped off with a nine-course meal from soup with eggplant dumplings to eggplant cake plus eggplant wine throughout.

In my own case, the exotic names of eggplant dishes enticed me and the actual flavors of the specialties won my affection.

Consider if you will names such as the *caponata* of Sicily, the *baba ghanouj* of Arabia, the *moussaka* of Greece, and the eggplant parmigiana of Italy.

How about the Turkish *iman bayeldi*, which means "the sultan fainted"? According to the legend, the sultan was a thrifty man who married a rich merchant's daughter. The bridegroom insisted that his wife's dowry include twelve huge jars of the best olive oil. One evening, the bride made an eggplant dish and her husband liked it so much, he ordered her to serve it every night. After twelve successive eggplant dinners, the bride balked and changed the menu. The iman was furious and demanded an explanation.

"My dear husband," the bride said, "in making your favorite dish, I have used all the oil I brought from my father's house. Now you will have to buy me a fresh supply."

The shock to the sultan's stomach and pocketbook made him faint, and ever since the dish — baked eggplant stuffed with tomatoes, garlic, sweet peppers, and onions — has been called *iman bayeldi.*

One night at dinner I heard the legend of the iman from Pat Lowther, who grew up in North Carolina and came to New Hampshire via Washington, the Peace Corps in Turkey, and teaching English in Zambia.

Eggplant is probably a native of Asia and was introduced to the Mediterranean peoples by the Arabs. When introduced to Italy, the vegetable was nicknamed *mala insana*, or raging apple, because some feared it would cause madness. Others declared the eggplant an aphrodisiac.

If you are wondering why a purple vegetable was named after an egg, you may not be aware that the vegetable comes in many colors as well as shapes. One variety grown in the Orient does indeed resemble a hen's egg; another variety is shaped like a cucumber; and still another, like a pumpkin. The other eggplant colors include white, deep green, maroon, and black.

When buying an eggplant, choose one with shiny skin and a bright green cap. Eggplants with shriveled dry caps are often old and bitter. Choose an eggplant that feels heavy and firm. Avoid those with wrinkles or bruises.

And strange as it seems, even the gentle eggplant is involved in several controversies aired in letters to the editors of large newspapers.

The first issue is whether to salt the eggplant slices to draw out the moisture — and according to some experts, the bitterness. James Beard says salting an eggplant is an old spouse's tale; if the vegetable is fresh, it is unnecessary. I prefer to avoid both the salt and the extra step.

The second issue has to do with gender. Some say if you want a sweeter eggplant with fewer seeds, select a male. Check the bottom of the vegetable where you will find a grayish scar or dimple. A round scar indicates a male. If the scar is oblong, the plant is female and full of seeds.

Nonsense, wrote a professor of medicine to *The New York Times.* "The edible portion of a tomato or an eggplant is composed of tissue derived from the female part of the flower. On this basis, even if not genetically accurate, one may assume all the eggplants are female."

Well, that may or may not be the last word.

But the next time you find a plump, firm eggplant and want to indulge yourself, consider making "poor man's caviar." This appetizer consists of roasted, chopped eggplant flavored with onions, tomatoes, lemon juice, anchovies, or tahini. The tiny seeds of the eggplant pulp may remind you of caviar grains. Just remember when you bake a whole eggplant to prick it a few times as you do a baking potato so the steam will escape. Otherwise, you may have a messy eggplant explosion to scrape off the sides of your oven.

If you have an extra raw eggplant, hollow it out and use it as the serving dish for "poor man's caviar."

The ultimate eggplant luxury is pickled baby eggplant. You can buy a jar of them along with real caviar at the fancy food shop. You could pickle your own, I suppose, but what kind of gardener harvests eggplants when they are the size of robins' eggs?

Only a gardener with an enormous amount of self-confidence could nip this chancy crop in the bud.

Caponata

Yield: 8 to 10 servings

½ cup olive oil
2 medium-size eggplants, peeled and sliced into 1-inch cubes
1 cup diced onion
1 cup diced celery
3 cups peeled, seeded, and chopped tomatoes
2 tablespoons sugar
¼ cup red wine vinegar
¼ cup capers, rinsed and drained
½ teaspoon freshly ground pepper
2 teaspoons dried basil
2 tablespoons tomato paste
1 tablespoon pine nuts

This is ratatouille's Sicilian cousin. Try to make it a day ahead of serving because caponata tastes better as the flavors mellow with age.

* * *

In a large, heavy saucepan, heat the olive oil over medium heat. Add the eggplants, onion, celery, and tomatoes. Cook over medium-low heat for about 20 minutes, or until the vegetables are just tender. Add the remaining ingredients, except the pine nuts. Cover and simmer for 15 minutes.

Stir in the pine nuts. Serve warm (not hot), at room temperature, or cold. This will keep in the refrigerator for about 2 weeks.

Palavi's Eggplant

Yield: 6 to 8 servings

1 large eggplant
1 tablespoon olive oil
1 small onion,
   chopped
½-inch piece fresh
   ginger root, pared
   and minced
¼ teaspoon ground
   cinnamon
¼ teaspoon ground
   nutmeg
¼ teaspoon ground
   ginger
¼ teaspoon ground
   cloves
1 cup plain yogurt
1 teaspoon dried mint
   leaves, crumbled
Fresh mint, for
   garnish

This can be served as a spread for plain crackers, as a dip for vegetables, or as an accompaniment to an Indian menu.

* * *

Preheat the oven to 350°F.

Place the unpeeled eggplant in a shallow pan. Make 6 incisions in the eggplant with the tip of a knife. Bake for 1 hour. Remove and cool. Split the cooled eggplant in half lengthwise and scoop out the flesh, discarding the skin. Mash the eggplant.

Heat the olive oil in a frying pan. Add the onion and ginger root and sauté until the onion is just translucent. Add the cinnamon, nutmeg, ginger, and cloves and cook for 1 minute.

Combine the eggplant, onion mixture, yogurt, and dried mint. Refrigerate for several hours or overnight. Garnish with a fresh mint sprig, if available, and serve.

Eggplant and Pasta Salad

Yield: 6 to 10 servings

1 large eggplant,
   peeled
¾ cup olive oil
¾ cup chopped onion
2 large garlic cloves,
   minced
3 tablespoons lemon
   juice
¾ teaspoon salt
⅛ teaspoon pepper
2 cups cooked pasta
   (shells, bows, or
   your choice)
2 large tomatoes,
   cubed (about 2½
   cups)
1 cup chopped fresh
   parsley
¾ cup sliced stuffed
   olives

Cut the eggplant into ½-inch cubes. In a large skillet, heat ¼ cup of the oil. Add the eggplant, onion, and garlic and sauté for 10 minutes until the vegetables are tender. Let the mixture cool to room temperature.

Mix the remaining ½ cup olive oil, lemon juice, salt, and pepper. Gently toss the oil mixture with the pasta, tomatoes, eggplant mixture, parsley, and olives. Cover and chill for several hours, stirring occasionally.

Eggplant Parmigiana

Yield: 8 servings

2 eggs
½ teaspoon dried
   oregano
½ teaspoon dried
   basil
1 garlic clove, minced
1 large eggplant
1 cup fine dried bread
   crumbs
Olive oil
4 cups seasoned
   tomato sauce
8 ounces thinly sliced
   mozzarella cheese
2 ounces freshly
   grated Parmesan
   cheese

The first parmigiana dish I made was veal. Then I discovered eggplant parmigiana. I began to prefer the eggplant version, because the vegetable is often available. Such is not the case with veal; one must have a connection somewhere behind the meat counter. On the rare occasions veal appears in the showcase, I prefer to make it piccata-style — sautéed with white wine and lemon.

* * *

Beat the eggs with the herbs and garlic. Peel the eggplant and slice ¼ inch thick. Dip the slices into egg, then into the bread crumbs.

Brown the eggplant quickly in heated olive oil. Some cooks use a skillet, but I prefer to spread a thin layer of oil on a large, shallow baking pan and let the eggplant brown in a 425°F. oven for 5 to 7 minutes on each side.

Reduce the oven temperature to 350°. Pour 1 cup tomato sauce into a 9-inch by 13-inch baking dish. Layer the eggplant on top of the tomato sauce. Cover with the cheeses. Pour the remaining tomato sauce on top. Bake for 30 minutes, or until bubbly. Let set for 10 minutes, then serve.

Chapter Six

Ripening

A s the summer matures and the vegetables ripen, the garden palette takes on intense colors. At the edges, deep purple cosmos and orange marigolds bloom at last. Scarlet tomatoes bursting with goodness inspire one more refreshing salad. Tomatoes that are not passionately consumed are canned for the seasons ahead.

Fresh corn, now cheaper by the dozen at the farm stand, pre-empts menus planned earlier in the day. Whether the best-tasting corn is deep gold or milky yellow is a matter of taste. All that really matters is that you eat the corn as soon as possible after it is picked. It is then that corn is the sweetest.

If the frost is due and most of your tomatoes are still green, perhaps your region had a cold, short gardening season. Or maybe you chose the wrong tomatoes for the local climate. The giant beefsteak tomato, for example, probably won't ever ripen in northern New England. But take heart, you can always make pickles out of green tomatoes.

Frost on the pumpkin won't hurt it a bit. In fact, the pumpkin can just sit and look pretty while you finish the preserving and freezing. After it has performed doorstop and centerpiece duty, your pumpkin can go on to a second career as a versatile edible.

Tomatoes and Taste Buds

If there is any hope for a mature American palate, it must be the Tomato Revolution.

No one has yet taken to the streets in outrage over tasteless tomatoes, nor has anyone dumped ethylene-ripened tomatoes into Boston Harbor. But as slowly and as imperceptibly as the constellations travel the night sky, people around me have begun to say no thank you to the orange pink balls packed in what is called a "cello tube." In the supermarket ads, these fruits are described with unintentional accuracy as "cello tomatoes."

I was surprised when Edward announced that he intended to quit eating these tomatoes. "I am going to wait until they come into season here," he said as he unpacked the groceries one January day. Now, it takes courage to renounce all Florida tomatoes six months before the first vine-ripened fruit appears in local markets.

Here is a man who, without question, dined for years from technology's table. Who knew any better? We squirted fake whipped cream onto ruby gelatin, spread imitation cheese on our crackers, and stirred sugar-dosed "lightener" into our instant coffee.

I have always found gassed tomatoes hard to swallow. When I was a girl, I helped my mother plant tomatoes in her Victory Garden. Every spring when I set out my seedlings, I think about that patriotic plot. The childhood memory surfaces when I handle a tomato seedling and it responds with the pungent aroma of tomato.

At harvest, my idea of ecstasy is standing in a garden patch eating a sun-warmed tomato. Alternate ecstasies of the season include a sandwich of homemade bread, tomato slices, fresh mayonnaise, a grind of pepper, and a ruffle of lettuce; or an uncooked tomato sauce flavored with garlic and basil served over hot pasta. The juxtaposition of temperatures is surprisingly refreshing to the palate — especially on a summer's night.

The American appetite for fresh tomatoes has made the fruit the most popular crop with backyard farmers. Even gardeners without a backyard grow cherry tomatoes in hanging pots and salad tomatoes in buckets on the terraces of city high-rises.

My neighbors swore off gardening entirely a few years ago when they began building a house and new careers. Out went the goats and the garden. They have relented since and now set out a half-dozen tomato plants and a row of basil every spring.

They don't even have to do that much, thanks to a renewed interest in fresh foods across the land. Even supermarkets make a point of carrying locally grown produce, and the nearby Saturday morning farmers' markets are flourishing.

Historically, Americans and tomatoes have had a curious relationship. The fruit, a native American, originated in the Andes. The Mayans were the first to cultivate the vines, and our word for the fruit comes from the Mayan word "tomatal." It wasn't until the sixteenth century that European traders introduced the tomato to Mediterranean countries. Can you imagine the cuisine of places like Athens, Rome, and Provence in pre-tomato times?

The French nicknamed it "the love apple" and believed it heightened sexual desire. Back on these shores, our ancestors declared the fruit poisonous. Thomas Jefferson planted and enjoyed the tomato and encouraged his neighbors to do likewise. By 1860, the widely circulated *Godey's Lady's Book* advised that tomatoes were edible "if stewed for at least three hours." In my opinion, stewed tomatoes are inedible.

Whether you say tuh-mah-toe or tuh-may-toe, the fruit's official name is *Lycopersicon esculentum*. The tomato belongs to the nightshade family. Some members of the family, such as belladonna, live up to their name, deadly nightshade. Happily, there is also an edible branch of the family, which includes peppers, tomatoes, eggplant, and potatoes. Perhaps the kinship explains why these flavors marry so well in dishes like ratatouille and eggplant parmigiana.

Although we often treat the fruit as if it were a vegetable, the tomato is actually a berry. That's because it has fleshy fruit, a thin skin, and seeds — but not a stone.

If you are looking for seasonings to combine with tomatoes, consider basil, bay leaf, chilies, curry, dill, garlic, mint, oregano, parsley, or thyme. One good cook tells me the secret of his Italian grandmother's spaghetti sauce is a pinch of ground cinnamon added with the traditional herbs.

The best tomatoes for making a thick spaghetti sauce are plum tomatoes. They are just one of the five hundred varieties of tomatoes available today. Other familiar types include the beefy salad tomato, the yellow tomato, and the cherry tomato.

The cherry tomato is available most of the year and adds a handy touch of color when you are serving an otherwise drab dish. People with patience slice off the top of a cherry tomato, scoop out the flesh with a grapefruit sectioner and a demitasse spoon, stuff it with crab meat or chicken salad, and serve it for an appetizer. I like to sauté the tiny tomatoes briefly and serve them atop a spring lamb ragout.

I feel about yellow tomatoes the same way I do yellow beets: They are an interesting variation, but I am content with the red version. Some cooks like yellow tomatoes for making marmalade and for alternating with sliced red tomatoes on a serving dish.

The thick flesh of the plum tomato makes it ideal for tomato paste. I delegate the paste making to the big growers, but I do can many quarts of the plum tomatoes every year. You can freeze them, but I prefer the taste of the canned tomatoes in cooking. Besides, there is a certain pleasure when the eye meets these treasures on the pantry shelf.

When I read about a fancy New York party where plum tomatoes were stuffed with goat cheese and chives and served as an appetizer, I was pleased that fresh foods continue to be fashionable.

Then I turned the page and read about scientists working with recombinant DNA to produce new kinds of tomatoes. One "improved" variety will have more meat and more flavor, the scientists predicted. The tomato will also be "candy apple red and square shaped for better packaging."

Just when I thought we were showing some sense.

Tomato Sauce

Yield: 5 cups

1 quart plum tomatoes
1 tablespoon olive oil
1 large onion, chopped
1 can (6 ounces) tomato paste
2 garlic cloves, minced
1 tablespoon dried basil or 6 fresh basil leaves, chopped
½ teaspoon dried oregano
½ teaspoon dried thyme
½ teaspoon dried marjoram
⅛ teaspoon ground cinnamon
1 teaspoon sugar

I started making this tomato sauce during the busiest part of the canning season. I doubled the recipe, filled the slow cooker, and let it cook while I attended to the rest of the harvest. When the sauce was cooked and cooled, I froze it in quart containers. I've since learned to freeze some in pint and half-pint containers for sauce to satisfy spontaneous pizza cravings. To make a meat sauce, add browned ground beef.

* * *

If you are using fresh tomatoes, plunge them briefly into boiling water to loosen the skins. Peel and chop the tomatoes into chunks. Place the tomatoes and their juice in a slow cooker. If you are using canned tomatoes, add the tomatoes and liquid from the can to the slow cooker.

Add the remaining ingredients and stir. Cook, uncovered, on high for 2 hours.

To freeze, cool and then pour into freezer containers, leaving 1 inch of head space at the top of the container for expansion. Label and freeze.

Tabouli or Parsley Salad

Yield: 6 to 8 servings

1 cup fine bulgur
(cracked wheat)
Boiling water
1 pound tomatoes,
peeled, seeded, and
chopped
2 cups chopped green
onions
3 cups chopped fresh
parsley
2 tablespoons fresh or
dried mint
½ cup olive oil
⅓ cup fresh lemon
juice
1 teaspoon salt
½ teaspoon freshly
ground black
pepper

I first discovered this refreshing salad when I lived in Jerusalem. Once I moved back to New England, I looked forward to making my own version straight from the garden. Recently, I saw this salad offered by its authentic name, Tabouli, *in a deli in Keene, New Hampshire. Somehow, I felt I had come full circle.*

* * *

Rinse the bulgur, cover with boiling water, and let stand for 30 minutes. Drain thoroughly and squeeze dry in a piece of cheesecloth or a clean dishtowel.

Combine the tomatoes, green onions, parsley, and mint in a large salad bowl. Beat together the oil, lemon juice, salt, and pepper. Fold into the tomato mixture. Mix in the bulgur until well blended. Cover and chill before serving.

Cucumber, Tomato, And Onion Salad

Yield: 4 to 6 servings

2 large, ripe tomatoes
2 cucumbers
1 sweet white or
Bermuda onion
½ cup Greek
kalamata olives
½ cup olive oil
¼ cup lemon juice
½ teaspoon fresh
oregano
2 teaspoons minced
fresh basil
Salt and freshly
ground pepper

Cut the tomatoes in half lengthwise and slice. Pare and slice the cucumbers. Peel the onion, slice, and separate into rings.

Arrange the vegetables attractively on a serving plate. Add the olives. Combine the oil, lemon juice, and herbs. Pour over the vegetables. Add salt and pepper to taste. Chill before serving.

Note: If you don't have fresh basil, substitute 1 teaspoon dried basil.

Fresh Tomato Sauce With Linguine

Yield: 4 servings

2 pounds tomatoes, peeled and coarsely chopped
2 garlic cloves, minced
½ cup coarsely chopped fresh basil leaves
¼ cup chopped fresh parsley
2 tablespoons finely chopped onion
½ cup plus 1 tablespoon olive oil
1 teaspoon sugar
Salt and freshly ground black pepper (optional)
1 pound linguine
Freshly grated Parmesan cheese

When I study seed catalogs in January, the memory of this fresh sauce is one reason I lose control in the tomato section. The combination of the room-temperature sauce and hot pasta is astonishingly delicious on an August night.

* * *

Combine the tomatoes, garlic, basil, parsley, onion, ½ cup olive oil, and sugar. Taste and add salt and pepper, if desired. Cover and let the flavors mature at room temperature for 3 hours before serving.

Cook the linguine according to the manufacturer's instructions. Add the remaining 1 tablespoon olive oil to the boiling water to prevent strands from sticking.

Drain the cooked linguine well and spoon on the tomato sauce. Sprinkle with Parmesan cheese and serve.

Let Us Celebrate Corn

When corn appears at the farmers' market, I am tempted to dance for joy. The impulse, it turns out, is not an original one. The Pueblos performed a corn dance every August. If they failed to dance, the Pueblos believed that the rains would not come, the stars would stand still, and the world would crumble.

These days, we need more dances, rituals, whatever, to let each other know we do not want to destroy the world. We want to continue our dances of joy for corn and every other living thing. We want to rejoice at the hand-lettered "native corn" signs announcing the arrival of the golden vegetable of August.

Some summer evenings, Edward and I make an entire meal of steamed corn on the cob. Our banquet consists of a platter of corn brushed with melted butter and dusted with freshly ground pepper.

When family and friends gather around our picnic table, we begin dinner at dusk with the corn and steamed clams or boiled lobster. We push away the darkness with the light of old kerosene lamps. Long after the blueberry pie is eaten, we are still at the table sipping wine and relishing good conversation. Edward and I are having the same thought: Perhaps our guests would be more comfortable inside the house.

But we don't move because there is something magical about our island of light. In the darkness beyond us, the creatures of the night go about their business in the meadow and forest. Do they, I wonder, observe us at the people feeder as we watch the birds at their bath?

Later, when my guests have departed, I sit by my garden and listen to the crickets. As the days grow shorter, the crickets intensify their canticle. I am reminded of a much-promoted remedy for corn-stealing raccoons. According to the experts, a radio placed among the stalks will keep away the raiders of the night.

But rather than filling the evening with country-and-western sounds from Wheeling, West Virginia, I delegate the growing of corn to a nearby farmer. For after-dark entertainment, I'll take the whippoorwills and owls.

When we have eaten our fill of fresh corn on the cob, I make corn chowder and an anchovy-flavored corn salad, a good dish for a picnic or buffet. I also put up a few jars of corn relish to add a bright touch to the winter table.

Three other kinds of corn extend the pleasures of the season: cornmeal, popcorn, and ornamental corn to decorate the door during autumn. Efficient people will welcome a variety called Strawberry Ornamental Popcorn. After the mahogany ears have done their decorating duty, the kernels can be popped for a snack. If you think stringing popcorn to hang on your Christmas tree is a novel idea, be aware that the American Indians used the white garlands for their religious feasts, too.

When I first began reading New England cookbooks, I was puzzled by three items — all having to do with cornmeal. First, it took me a while to figure out what Indian meal was. Then it occurred to me that Yankees called corn grain Indian meal because they first learned about it from the native Americans.

I was also mystified by references to gem pans and spider cakes. Gems are corn muffins baked in a special cast-iron pan. They are shaped like an old-fashioned gem or like a Twinkie sliced horizontally. A spider is a cast-iron skillet with long legs that allow it to be placed on fireplace coals. Today's spider cake is still baked in a skillet, but it contains nothing more exotic than cornmeal, eggs, and buttermilk.

The name of one kind of corncake is still a source of controversy, according to upcountry radio call-in shows. Each caller insists one of three names — johnnycake, journey cake, or Shawnee cake — is the official name. The cake itself is pretty bland and hardly worth the argument.

We can thank the Incas and the Aztecs for nearly one thousand varieties of corn. Originally, wild corn was a grass growing in the Andes. Its cob was the size of a blade of wheat. The native Americans developed the gold and silver varieties of field corn, as well as the red and blue meal corn of the Southwest.

I wonder what those ancient horticulturists would think of a report from the Corn Producers Association. The president of the association reported that corn in the form of oil, starch, or sweeteners is now present in 1,276 different foods. The corn products, he said, "preserve moisture, provide energy and flavor, control crystal formation, improve texture and color, and maintain firmness and freshness in such foods as low-calorie dinners, yogurt, ice cream sandwich bars, frozen desserts, delicatessen meats, and baked goods."

Somehow, that news made me long for an ear of corn roasted the Indian way. No foil, no roasting bags, no seasoned coating. Just an ear of corn baking away in its own water-soaked husk over the coals.

Brian's Chicken Corn Chowder

Yield: 4 to 6 servings

1 whole chicken
   breast, split
3 cups water
4 tablespoons butter
1 large onion,
   chopped
4 tablespoons flour
½ teaspoon
   Worcestershire
   sauce
1½ cups fresh corn
   kernels or 1
   package (10
   ounces) frozen corn
   kernels
1 chicken bouillon
   cube
2 cups milk, scalded
Paprika

This chicken corn chowder makes a fine weekend lunch or supper. Serve with a hot bread and fruit for dessert.

* * *

Simmer the chicken breast in the water for 22 to 25 minutes. Reserve the broth. Cool the chicken, discard the skin, and cut the meat into bite-size pieces.

In a large saucepan, melt the butter. Add the onion and cook over low heat until the onion is translucent. Sprinkle the flour on the onion and cook and stir for 3 minutes. Gradually add the reserved chicken broth and cook and stir for 3 minutes. Add the Worcestershire sauce, corn, and bouillon cube and simmer for 5 minutes.

Add the chicken and stir in the milk. Cook and stir just until the mixture begins to boil. Serve in chowder bowls and dust lightly with paprika.

Corn Salad With Anchovy Dressing

Yield: 6 to 8 servings

1 cup salad oil
¼ cup vinegar
6 anchovy fillets, coarsely chopped
4 cups fresh or frozen corn kernels
½ cup pitted, sliced black olives
½ cup minced onion
1 sweet red pepper, seeded and chopped
2 tablespoons chopped fresh parsley, for garnish

I was surprised when guests asked me for the recipe for this corn salad. The occasion was the first buffet dinner I gave. I was young and innocent and invited 20 people. The other dishes on the menu were complicated and time-consuming to make, but this was the favorite. It can be prepared in advance and also travels well to pot-luck dinners.

* * *

In a blender, whirl the oil, vinegar, and anchovies until well mixed.

If you are using frozen corn, refresh it under cold water and drain. Mix the corn, olives, onion, and red pepper. Toss with the dressing. Refrigerate for at least 2 hours before serving. Drain before serving and use the extra dressing for the next day's salad. Garnish with the parsley.

Note: Drained canned corn can be substituted for the fresh or frozen. A jar (2 ounces) of pimiento can be substituted for the red pepper.

New England Corn Fritters

Yield: 4 servings

1 egg, beaten
½ cup milk
1 cup unbleached all-purpose flour
2 teaspoons baking powder
½ teaspoon salt
1 cup cream-style corn
2 tablespoons soft shortening
1 tablespoon grated onion (optional)
Melted butter
Warm pure maple syrup

At dinner, when a saucer of corn fritters and maple syrup appears unannounced on the table of a New England inn, you can hear the visitors from the big city sigh with pleasure.

* * *

Combine the egg, milk, flour, baking powder, salt, corn, shortening, and onion (if desired). Beat until thoroughly mixed. Drop by large spoonfuls onto a well-greased griddle or frying pan. When bubbles appear on the surface, turn and brown on the other side.

Serve with the melted butter and warmed maple syrup. Fritters are great to serve with roast turkey, chicken, or ham.

Bessie's Corn Relish

Yield: Approximately 5 half-pint jars

12 ears corn
2 onions, chopped
2 sweet green peppers, seeded and chopped
1 sweet red pepper, seeded and chopped
1 cup sliced celery
2 tablespoons pickling salt
2 tablespoons mustard seeds
1 cup sugar
1 cup cider vinegar

This colorful favorite is traditionally served with baked beans and brown bread.

* * *

Cut the kernels from the corn. Place the vegetables in a large kettle. Mix the salt, mustard seeds, sugar, and vinegar. Pour into the kettle. Bring to a boil; then lower the heat and simmer for 20 minutes.

Pour into hot, sterilized half-pint jars leaving ¼ inch head space. Seal. Process in a boiling water bath for 5 minutes. Cool and store in a cool, dry place.

What to Do with Green Tomatoes

If you think your neighbor the gardener is generous with zucchini and cucumbers, just hint for a few green tomatoes.

Do it when the time is ripe — say the night before a killing frost is predicted — and you will be rewarded with more tomatoes than you can cope with.

If you haven't a clue when a frost is due, begin watching your neighbor's garden in early September. When shower curtains and sleeping bags blossom where vines once grew, the moment is here. Your neighbors are buying time with bed sheets. By covering the less hardy plants for a night or two, they can delay doing something about the tomato overload for two or three weeks. Doing something involves canning and freezing, and that means work.

At this point, your friends are tired, tired, tired of tomatoes — red and green. After all, the seeds were ordered during a January blizzard, started on town meeting day in March, set out on Memorial Day, and nursed through cutworms and hornworms. Can you blame your neighbors for wanting to pitch a few bushels your way?

Now, what can you do with such a windfall? First, avoid two perennial bits of advice from well-meaning people.

Don't pull up the plants and hang the tomato-laden vines on a garage wall to ripen. You'll have to sweep up soil and leaves, and every now and then a tomato will zing down and burst upon you or your car.

Don't bother wrapping green tomatoes in newspaper. It's one of those chores you must keep doing. To check its progress, each tomato must be unwrapped and rewrapped several times. If you are ripening six dozen tomatoes, it won't be long before you quit checking. Then your nose will reveal when the fruit is ripe, and it will be too late.

Instead, place the best of the green tomatoes — discard any with brown spots or cracks — in single layers in shallow trays or cartons lined with plastic. An unopened trash bag makes a good liner. Place the trays away from direct sunlight in a cool room, and cover each tray with newspaper to harness the ethylene gas generated by the fruit. The paper traps the gas and hastens ripening. Cover the tomatoes loosely because, like human beings, they need oxygen to breathe. Using this method, I have stretched a fresh tomato supply through November.

There is a new tomato variety called Long Keeper that is planted late in the season and will supply the gardener with fresh tomatoes until mid-January. But I never plan that far ahead. In fact, I prefer to resolve the whole business quickly by making relishes, pickles, mincemeat, and chutney.

My neighbor, whose ancestors are French-Canadian, taught me about fried green tomatoes. She dips thick slices of green tomatoes into seasoned cornmeal or flour and frys them in oil or bacon fat until lightly browned.

Consider sautéing chopped green tomatoes with onions and seasoning them with curry powder. Other popular green tomato recipes include pie, spice cake, cookies, and candied fruit to be used like citron.

One of my favorite recipes was a gift from a thrifty friend, Marjorie Graves. I was mourning the loss of my cucumber crop to a drought when she offered me a recipe for green tomato relish. By the time I serve the relish with hot dogs or hamburgers, I have forgotten about the green tomatoes. And so far no one else has noticed the absence of cucumbers. The recipe calls for using a hand-turned meat grinder to chop the ingredients, but you can use a food processor if you pay close attention. Instead of tying spices in cheese-cloth, I prefer to put them in a tea ball. This cuts down on the number of runaway mustard seeds and peppercorns seeking their own level and finding a permanent home between the wide pine boards of my ancient kitchen.

Marjorie's Green Tomato Relish

Yield: Approximately 6 pints

24 green tomatoes
4 large onions
3 green peppers
3 sweet red peppers
3 tablespoons pickling salt
3 cups sugar
3 tablespoons mixed pickling spices, tied in a cloth
3 cups white distilled vinegar

Finely chop the tomatoes, onions, and peppers. You may use a food processor to chop the vegetables. Use the pulsing action so that the vegetables will be finely chopped but not puréed. Add the pickling salt to the vegetables and let stand for 1 hour. Then drain and add the remaining ingredients. Boil slowly for 1 hour.

Pack the relish into hot, sterilized pint jars, leaving ¼ inch head space. Seal and process for 5 minutes in a boiling water bath. Cool and store in a cool, dry place.

Geraldine Hall's Green Tomato Mincemeat

Yield: Approximately 6 pints

2 pounds green tomatoes
Water
2 pounds peeled, cored, and chopped apples
1½ pounds chopped raisins
1 pound chopped suet
1½ teaspoons salt
1½ tablespoons ground cinnamon
2 teaspoons ground cloves
2 teaspoons ground nutmeg
Grated rind and juice of 2 lemons
3½ pounds brown sugar

When I was searching for a good recipe for green tomato mincemeat, my good friend and colleague, Arlie Corday, offered her mother's. Mrs. Hall lives in Redfield, New York, where she and her husband have farmed and raised 9 fine children. She says margarine can be substituted for suet in the following recipe and suggests the mincemeat be used to make filled cookies.

* * *

Wash and dry the tomatoes. Finely chop, using a food grinder, chopper, or processor. Drain thoroughly. Add 2 cups of water and bring to a boil. Drain the tomatoes, reserving the liquid to measure. Discard the liquid and add an equal amount of fresh water. Repeat the process. Add the remaining ingredients, along with the fresh water, to the tomatoes. Simmer for 1 hour. Cool and store in pint containers in the refrigerator or freezer.

Zingy Green Tomato And Apple Relish

Yield: 9 pints

8 tart red apples
6 pounds green
   tomatoes
6 sweet red peppers
8 onions
1 small hot pepper
3 tablespoons pickling
   salt
1 tablespoon ground
   cinnamon
1½ teaspoons ground
   cloves
5 cups sugar
1 quart cider vinegar

Gladys Manyan is a friend and colleague whom I have yet to meet. She writes a food column for The Concord (New Hampshire) Monitor, *and we visit occasionally by telephone or letter. Like most of her readers, I have come to know this special woman through* The Country Seasons Cookbook *(Crown). In it, she describes a lifestyle I know so well: City innocent moves to ancient New England farm, struggles, and then to her own surprise, flourishes. This is one of Mrs. Manyan's solutions to the green tomato surplus.*

* * *

Core the apples, but do not peel them. Put the vegetables and apples through the coarse blade of a food chopper. Combine the other ingredients in a large enamel or stainless steel pot and bring to a boil. Add the vegetables and apples and simmer for 20 minutes, stirring occasionally. Pack in hot, sterilized pint jars, leaving ¼ inch head space. Seal. Process for 5 minutes in a boiling water bath. Cool and store in a cool, dry place.

A Note from Mrs. Manyan: "When putting vegetables and apples through the food chopper, I spread newspaper on the floor and set a glass bowl under the chopper to catch the juices. I return all the juices to the mixture except the green tomato juice, which I discard to prevent the relish from being too soupy. If you can't find red peppers, use green."

Green Tomato Dill Pickles

Yield: 6 quarts

1½ quarts white
distilled vinegar
1½ cups pickling salt
4½ quarts boiling
water
72 green tomatoes,
each the size of a
Ping-Pong ball or
smaller
2 large bunches fresh
dill
2 large garlic cloves,
quartered
6 fresh grape leaves

Have you ever seen a jar of green tomato pickles on a deli counter next to the pickled eggs? Here's the recipe for making them at home.

* * *

Combine the vinegar, pickling salt, and water and bring to a boil. Simmer the brine gently for 5 minutes.

Wash and drain the tomatoes.

Place a sprig of dill in the bottom of each of 6 hot, sterilized quart canning jars. Fill the jars with the tomatoes. To each jar, add a garlic quarter. Fill the jar to within ½ inch of the top with the vinegar mixture. Top with a grape leaf.

Seal and process for 10 minutes in a boiling water bath. Cool and store in a cool, dry place.

Pumpkin:
Pride of the Patch

Pumpkins are pure pleasure for the New England gardener. About the first of June, you plop a few pumpkinseeds into the ground. The seeds are large and easy to handle — unlike the persnickety and microscopic carrot and lettuce seeds. If the pumpkinseeds never come up, that's okay with most gardeners because the fruits are not as crucial to winter menus as are the onions, tomatoes, and peppers. If the seeds sprout, the pumpkin vines demand little attention, for they have few predators. Their presence in the garden is a relaxed one. Unlike the green beans, a pumpkin won't shout "pickle me" or "freeze me" every time you pass the plot on your way to the beach.

No, a pumpkin just sits benignly in the patch waiting for its day. Its day comes when the rest of the world turns gold. When the gold-leafed sugar maple filters the October sunlight as it floods the meadows. When the evening sky is streaked with gold lights bouncing off trees covering the hills.

The time of the pumpkin brings a smile to my face when I remember the folk tales of childhood. There was Cinderella flying through the night in a pumpkin coach. Peter the Pumpkin Eater stored his wife in a pumpkin shell. And the ghost in Washington Irving's "The Legend of Sleepy Hollow" had a pumpkin for its head.

Closer to home, we have the marvelous legend of the Racer Pumpkins of the Connecticut River valley. These huge pumpkins escaped from the field of a Massachusetts farmer and raced up the valley like a litter of piglets. They put down roots for a few days at a time in New Hampshire towns, such as Hinsdale and Winchester, and then gathered their vines and raced north once more.

Nine thousand years ago, pumpkins were cultivated in the Mexican highlands.

The Indians who befriended the Pilgrims taught them to bake, fry, and boil pumpkin pulp. They also taught them to make bread from pumpkins and to dry the pulp for a winter soup. The colonists mashed the pumpkin and mixed it with maple syrup for a home-brew.

Henry David Thoreau was among the pumpkin sitters of the nineteenth century. "I would rather sit on a pumpkin and have it all to myself than be crowded on a velvet cushion," he wrote.

The pumpkin is a member of the cucurbit (gourd) family, as are the summer and winter squashes. You can substitute a winter squash, such as Hubbard or butternut, for the pumpkin in a recipe.

Pumpkin pickers should know there are two kinds of pumpkins — one is good eating, as they say in northern New England, and the other is good for jack-or-jill-o'-lanterns. For pies, I grow the varieties Small Sugar or New England Pie. To light up the night with a lantern, you can grow such varieties as Big Max or the Connecticut Field pumpkins.

If you are a competitive person, you can enter your prize pumpkin in the Grand International Pumpkinship at Half Moon Bay, California. Perhaps Half Moon Bayers need something to keep them busy at this time of year. In New England, we are putting up storm windows and planting a snow shovel at each end of the driveway.

Even so, the last time I checked the pumpkinship title, it had been captured by a gardener from Nova Scotia whose pumpkin weighed 391 pounds.

As for me, I am content to eat my pumpkin flavored with cinnamon, cloves, maple syrup, and walnuts. However, if you are looking for other ways to use pumpkin, consider making it into pickles or putting the fruit in a mousse, in a sauce for lamb or veal, or in cheesecake.

And yes, if anyone asks, tell him a pumpkin is a fruit, not a vegetable. If your favorite food has seeds, then botanically, it is a fruit. And that includes cucumbers and squash.

Here are some favorites to enjoy while waiting for the arrival of The Great Pumpkin.

Pumpkin Soup

Yield: 6 to 8 servings

2 tablespoons butter
¼ cup chopped onion
6 cups chicken broth
3 cups cooked
   pumpkin purée
¼ teaspoon ground
   ginger
¼ teaspoon ground
   cloves
1 cup heavy cream
Salt
Freshly ground black
   pepper
¼ cup dry sherry

Heat the butter in a heavy saucepan and sauté the onion until it is translucent. Stir in the chicken broth, pumpkin, and spices. Continue stirring and bring to a boil. Lower the heat and simmer for 20 minutes, stirring occasionally.

If you prefer a very smooth soup, put the pumpkin mixture through a food mill or whirl in a blender at this point.

Return the mixture to the saucepan. Add the cream and adjust the seasonings to taste. Add the sherry and carefully bring the soup to a boil. Serve immediately or chill and serve cold.

Note: If you use fresh pumpkin, remember that 1 pound of raw peeled pumpkin will make about 4 cups of cubed pumpkin to yield 2 cups of cooked pumpkin purée. After cooking, drain well and put through a food mill or food processor before using.

Pumpkin Cookies

Yield: 3 dozen cookies

2½ cups cake flour
4 teaspoons baking
   powder
¼ teaspoon ground
   ginger
½ teaspoon ground
   nutmeg
½ teaspoon ground
   cinnamon
½ cup butter or
   margarine
1¼ cups firmly
   packed brown sugar
2 eggs
1½ cups cooked
   pumpkin purée
1 cup raisins
1 cup chopped nuts
1 tablespoon fresh
   lemon juice

Preheat the oven to 375°F.

Sift together the flour, baking powder, and spices. Set aside.

Cream the butter or margarine and brown sugar thoroughly. Add the eggs and pumpkin. Blend well.

Stir the raisins and nuts into the flour mixture. Add the flour mixture to the creamed mixture and beat. Stir in the lemon juice.

Drop from a teaspoon onto a greased cookie sheet. Bake for 12 to 15 minutes, or until lightly browned. Remove from the pan and cool on wire racks.

Pumpkin Chiffon Pie

Yield: 6 servings

1 envelope (1 tablespoon) unflavored gelatin
¾ cup firmly packed dark brown sugar
½ teaspoon ground nutmeg
½ teaspoon ground ginger
½ teaspoon ground cinnamon
¼ teaspoon ground cloves
½ cup milk
2 cups cooked pumpkin purée
2 eggs, separated
½ cup whipping cream
⅓ cup white sugar
1 baked 9-inch graham cracker crust
Whipped cream, for garnish
Candied ginger, for garnish

In a heavy saucepan, combine the gelatin, brown sugar, spices, milk, pumpkin, and beaten egg yolks. Bring to a boil, stirring constantly. Remove from the heat and cool.

Beat the egg whites until stiff and fold gently into the cooled pumpkin mixture.

Whip the cream until thick, gradually add the white sugar, and beat until stiff. Fold the whipped cream into the pumpkin mixture.

Pour the pumpkin mixture into the crust and refrigerate until set, about 3 hours. Garnish with whipped cream and bits of candied ginger.

Apple Brandy Pumpkin Mousse

Yield: 4 to 5 servings

¼ cup calvados or
  applejack
1 envelope (1
  tablespoon)
  unflavored gelatin
4 eggs
7 tablespoons sugar
1 cup cooked
  pumpkin purée
½ teaspoon ground
  cinnamon
¼ teaspoon ground
  ginger
¼ teaspoon ground
  nutmeg
1 cup heavy cream

Place the calvados or applejack in the top of a small double boiler. Sprinkle the gelatin over the brandy to soften. Place the pan over simmering water and stir until the gelatin is dissolved.

Place the eggs in a large bowl and beat, adding the sugar gradually. Beat until mixture is light colored and very thick.

Combine the pumpkin and the spices and stir into the eggs. Add the brandy mixture and blend well.

In a separate bowl, whip the cream into soft peaks. Fold into the pumpkin mixture.

Pour into 4 or 5 dessert dishes or a large serving bowl. Chill for 4 hours before serving.

Stuffed Pumpkin

Yield: 8 servings

1 small pumpkin, 8 to
  10 inches in
  diameter
Boiling water
2 pounds ground beef
2 tablespoons
  vegetable oil
½ cup finely chopped
  green pepper
1 cup finely chopped
  onion
2 garlic cloves,
  minced
2 teaspoons dried
  oregano
1 teaspoon white
  distilled vinegar
1 cup raisins
1 cup seasoned
  tomato sauce
½ cup dry red wine or
  cider
Salt and freshly
  ground black
  pepper
3 eggs, beaten

Using a sharp knife, cut a circular top 5 inches in diameter from the top of the pumpkin. Reserve the top to use as a lid. Scoop out the seeds and strings from inside the pumpkin.

Place the pumpkin in a large kettle and cover with boiling water. Cover the kettle, bring the water to a boil, lower the heat, and simmer the pumpkin for about 30 minutes, or until the meat is almost tender. The pumpkin should remain firm enough to hold its shape.

Carefully remove the pumpkin from the water and drain well. Set aside.

Brown the ground beef in a large, heavy skillet until the meat loses its redness. Drain the fat from the meat and discard. Remove the meat to a bowl. Heat the oil in the skillet and add the green pepper, onion, and garlic. Sauté just until soft. Return the meat to the skillet and add the oregano, vinegar, raisins, tomato sauce, and wine or cider. Add salt and pepper to taste. Cover the skillet and simmer the mixture for 15 minutes, stirring occasionally. Cool slightly and add the eggs, mixing thoroughly.

Preheat the oven to 350°F.

Fill the pumpkin with stuffing, pressing to pack firmly.

Top loosely with the pumpkin lid and place in a greased shallow baking pan. Bake for 1 hour. Cool for 15 minutes before serving.

To serve, carefully transfer the pumpkin to a serving platter. Slice into 8 wedges.

Chapter Seven

Foliage Season

T he autumn air is so clean, so crisp that it crackles with energy. The haze, humidity, and summer people disappeared around Labor Day. Now come the visitors from other parts of this country and the world. They are here to witness the foliage spectacle. We who live here never grow complacent about the stunning red, orange, and gold leaves of autumn. Or the evening light that shines pink and then purple on the foliage.

The house guests who arrive in this season catch me as my cooking mood quickens. The harvest is in and my freezer is as full as a supermarket shelf. Jars of plum tomatoes, Concord grape juice, and pickles add rich color to the pantry shelves. I am eager and proud to share my treasures.

The time of the apple and the cider has arrived. One advantage of going to the orchard to pick your own apples is the perfume. I doubt even one of the greats like Chanel could have created that effect — not to mention the seductive aroma of a cinnamon-scented apple chutney bubbling on the back of the stove.

Lunch for the Leaf Peepers

An autumn lunch by the fireplace is a simple but satisfying way to entertain the city folks who come up our way to drink in the annual foliage splendor.

I like to prepare everything ahead of time, so when our guests arrive, we can spend all of our time with them. And nothing is lost if our friends are delayed by an impulse to go antiquing or if the driver misses the fork leading to the dirt road that winds up the hill to our house.

One of my favorite menus includes a hearty lentil soup, whole wheat bread, raw vegetables (including the sweet carrots just pulled from what is left of the garden), a beverage, and fruit and cheese for dessert. When I am not dieting, I serve homemade chocolate chip or oatmeal cookies with dessert.

I make the cookies, the bread, and the soup the night before. The soup certainly improves as it ages. The bread is made by the "cool-rise method" developed by the Robin Hood Flour Company. This method works out well for the person who has limited time to bake bread. The dough can be mixed within an hour and rises overnight in the refrigerator.

Like most other northern New Englanders who live in old country houses, I have discovered there are few, if any, places in my house that reach a dough-rising 85°F. between November and April. There may be one such spot in our house between the chimney and potbellied stove. But I will never know. A pair of resident felines has appropriated the space.

In any case, the refrigerator-rise method works for me. Frequently, I multiply the recipe by three to make six loaves. I do this on a Friday night when the refrigerator is likely to be empty, and I bake it on Saturday morning when we have time to enjoy the aroma of baking bread. I slice the remaining loaves when they are cooled and stash them in the freezer.

The morning of the foliage lunch, I prepare the vegetables, assemble them on a serving dish, cover it with plastic wrap, and store in the refrigerator. I bake the bread and chill the wine. A Chenin Blanc is nice with this menu. Or you can serve cider or an apple-flavored tea.

For dessert, I serve local apples. And city dwellers always appreciate Vermont cheddar cheese.

Honey Lemon
Whole Wheat Bread

Yield: 2 loaves

**3¼ to 4¼ cups
unbleached all-
purpose flour
2 packages (scant
tablespoon each)
active dry yeast
1 tablespoon salt
¼ cup honey
3 tablespoons
softened margarine
or shortening
1 tablespoon grated
lemon rind
2¼ cups hot water
2 cups whole wheat
flour
Vegetable oil**

Combine 2 cups of the all-purpose flour, the yeast, and salt in a large bowl. Stir well. Add the honey, margarine or shortening, and lemon rind. Add the water all at once.

Beat with an electric mixer at medium speed for 1 minute. Stir in the whole wheat flour with a wooden spoon. Stir in just enough of the remaining all-purpose flour to make a soft dough that leaves the sides of the bowl.

Turn onto a floured board and round up into a ball. Knead for 5 to 10 minutes until the dough is smooth and elastic. Cover with a towel. Let the dough rest for 20 minutes. Punch down.

Divide the dough in half. Roll each half into an 8-inch by 12-inch rectangle. Roll up tightly into loaves beginning at the 8-inch side. Seal the edges and ends. Tuck the ends under.

Place into greased 4½-inch by 8½-inch by 2½-inch loaf pans. Brush the surface of the dough with oil. Cover the pans loosely with waxed paper. Refrigerate the loaves from 2 to 24 hours. When you are ready to bake, remove from the refrigerator. Uncover the pans and set the oven at 400°F. Puncture any air bubbles on the surface of the loaves with a toothpick.

Bake for 30 to 40 minutes, or until the loaves are golden brown and sound hollow when tapped. Bake on the lowest oven rack for best results.

Remove from the pans immediately after taking from oven. Cool on racks.

Classic Lentil Soup

Yield: 8 to 10 servings

¼ cup olive oil
1 cup chopped onion
1 cup chopped green
  pepper
3 garlic cloves,
  chopped
1 pound uncooked
  lentils
1 cup sliced celery
1 cup sliced carrots
1 can (16 ounces)
  plum tomatoes,
  with liquid
1 bay leaf
½ teaspoon dried
  thyme
8 cups water
Salt and freshly
  ground black
  pepper
2 tablespoons fresh
  lemon juice

Heat the olive oil in a frying pan. Add the onion, green pepper, and garlic and sauté until soft. Pour into a deep pot or Dutch oven.

Add the lentils, celery, carrots, tomatoes, bay leaf, thyme, and water. Heat to boiling. Reduce the heat. Simmer until the lentils are very soft, about 1 hour.

Taste and add salt and pepper. Stir in the lemon juice and serve.

Tani's Sabra Dessert

Yield: 8 to 10 servings

½ gallon real vanilla
  ice cream
1½ ounces Sabra
  (chocolate-orange
  liqueur)
2 teaspoons freshly
  grated orange rind
Hershey's chocolate
  syrup
Grated chocolate, for
  garnish

"This is my special secret for people like me who always have last-minute guests," says Tani Leach. She learned the formula in cooking school and says it can be varied with bourbon or other spirits.

* * *

Pile the ice cream into a food processor; it will hold more than you think. Add the Sabra, orange rind, and chocolate syrup to taste. Whirl until the mixture is the consistency of a very thick milkshake. Serve in stemmed glasses and garnish with grated chocolate.

Note: Tani says she starts with ½ gallon of ice cream. You may not need to use it all. Sabra liqueur is a combination of bitter oranges and Swiss chocolate.

Apple Orchard Tea

Yield: 8 servings

1 quart water
6 tea bags or 2
   tablespoons loose
   tea leaves
¼ cup sugar
1 cup apple juice
2 tablespoons lemon
   juice

Bring the water to a full rolling boil. Pour over the tea. Brew for 3 to 5 minutes. Remove the tea bags or strain. Add the sugar and stir until dissolved. Add the apple and lemon juices. Serve immediately.

The Black Walnut Plantation

" Fill your pockets," said kindly Farmer Hicks of Batavia, New York. Obedient child that I was, I scooped up every fruit I could find under the majestic black walnut tree.

I could not know I was repeating a rite of autumn performed by native Americans as they gathered food for the winter. I could not yet appreciate that this very tree may have nourished generations of Tuscarora or Chippewa Indians.

With the limited vision of a child, I was pleased a great war in distant places had ended. That meant once again there was gasoline for leisurely Sunday drives to the country. My father preferred buying his apples, potatoes, and onions from the man who grew them.

Back home, I spread my walnuts on the sidewalk and attacked them with a hammer. To free the meat, I had to use force to remove both the husk and the shell. I was not dealing with the mild-flavored English walnut (*Juglans regia*), which readily yields its contents to the squeeze of a nutcracker. This was the reluctant *Juglans nigra*. Like the lobster, this nut demands more effort and, correspondingly, grants a greater pleasure.

There are those who hold that black walnuts are an acquired taste, like rhubarb or pickled pigs' feet. Not the usual childish fare. It is true my youthful tastes ran to imitation banana-flavored taffy. But I still fell in love with the earthy black walnut. Or perhaps it was the memory of a radiant October afternoon.

When we moved to New Hampshire, I planted bridal wreath, bleeding hearts, and hydrangeas. Edward began cultivating the forest and planting trees. He recited a long list of seedlings available from the state for a few pennies apiece. Never mind the Norway spruce and the fir balsam; all I heard was black walnuts.

Imagine never buying outrageously priced nuts. Picture a pantry stocked with every ingredient for a spontaneous batch of cookies or fudge.

The state foresters had something else in mind: If the tree's natural growing range could be extended beyond the Midwest, the amount of valuable timber produced could be increased.

The fine-grained wood of the black walnut makes exquisite furniture and cabinetry. Its rich color needs only a clear finish. This wood is used for the gunstocks of the arms we supply to nearly every nation on earth. One forest handbook notes, "No other wood has served the world so well in times of peace and in times of distress." Another manual warns about the theft of entire trees by rustlers in helicopters. The trunks can be sold for up to five-figure sums.

Susan Norlander, an artist who lives in Alstead, New Hampshire, uses black walnut husks to color the wool clipped from the sheep she raises. The dye from the husks — unlike most dyes — needs no mordant to fix the color. And the resulting yarn is the color of butterscotch caramels.

Susan once lived in Indiana, the heart of black walnut country, and she remembers the bup-bup-bup song made by the trees as they released their fruits.

After we planted our seedlings, I recall the county forester telling us the trees would bear fruit in about three years. I collected recipes for black walnut ice cream, Pennsylvania Christmas cake, and black walnut fudge. I squirreled away tips about driving a car over the husks to free the nut. My files became full with notes on the how-tos of shelling, such as freezing the nuts or soaking them in water for days before attacking them with a hammer.

I collected lore about both black and English walnuts, which are more correctly called Persian walnuts. The walnut tree appears in the Unicorn Tapestries, some of which hang in The Cloisters Museum in New York City. The tapestries were woven in the Middle Ages using silk and wool yarns. The unknown French or Flemish artist filled the background of the wall-size hangings with what were considered the most beautiful plants in existence. At the time, the walnut tree was a symbol of durability.

Durability is an essential quality for walnut farmers. Eighteen springs have passed since we planted our seedlings, and we have yet to harvest a single nut from the healthy saplings.

These days, when a recipe calls for black walnuts, I substitute the English kind. I learned to do this when the walnut plantation entered its fourth year. But I continue to fatten a file folder of recipes for the *Juglans nigra*. Edward predicts the nuts will appear in our grove any autumn now. Meanwhile, Lucy, the energetic kitten, regularly uses the teenage trees for her jungle gym.

Chicken Salad With 5-2-2-1 Dressing

Yield: 6 to 8 servings

4 quarts water
3 pounds whole
  boneless chicken
  breasts
2 cups pineapple
  chunks
1 cup green grapes
½ cup coarsely
  chopped walnuts
¼ teaspoon ground
  ginger
1 recipe 5-2-2-1
  Dressing (recipe
  follows)
Salt and pepper
  (optional)
Lettuce or other
  greens

Bring the water to a boil. Add the chicken and reduce the heat to a simmer. Simmer for 20 minutes. Remove the pan from the heat and let the chicken cool in the broth.

Remove the chicken from the broth and reserve the broth for a soup or sauce. Discard the skin and cut the chicken into bite-size pieces. Add the pineapple, grapes, walnuts, and ginger to the chicken and toss lightly. Add the dressing and mix lightly. Taste and add salt and pepper, if desired. Chill. Serve on a bed of greens.

5-2-2-1 Dressing

Yield: Approximately ⅔ cup

5 tablespoons salad
  oil
2 tablespoons white
  distilled vinegar
2 tablespoons Dijon-
  style mustard
1 tablespoon lemon
  juice
1 tablespoon honey
  (optional)
1 tablespoon poppy
  seeds (optional)

Whisk the oil, vinegar, mustard, and lemon juice until mixed. Add the honey and poppy seeds, if desired.

Stella Kiritsy's Walnut Cake   *Yield: About 25 servings*

8 eggs, separated
1⅓ cups sugar
1½ teaspoons baking
  powder
¾ teaspoon ground
  cinnamon
2 cups ground walnuts
1 cup crushed
  zwieback
⅓ cup water
2 tablespoons lemon
  juice
Thin slices of lemon,
  for garnish

When the women of the local Greek church sponsor their Christmas fair, the pastries are quickly sold out. This cake, called karidopita, *is one of the favorites.*

* * *

Preheat the oven to 350°F.

In a small bowl, beat together the egg yolks and 1 cup of the sugar, using an electric mixer on high for about 5 minutes. Stir in the baking powder and cinnamon.

Wash the beaters. Beat the egg whites until stiff in a large bowl.

In another bowl, mix the walnuts and the zwieback.

Fold the egg yolks into the egg whites. Fold in the walnut-zwieback mixture. Pour into a greased 9-inch by 13-inch baking pan. Bake for 30 to 35 minutes, or until a toothpick inserted in the center comes out clean.

Meanwhile, mix the water, the remaining ⅓ cup sugar, and the lemon juice in a small saucepan. Bring to a boil and simmer gently for 10 minutes. Cool.

Pour the cold syrup on the cake as soon as it comes out of the oven. Let the cake rest for several hours and then cut into diamonds. Halve the lemon slices and garnish the cake. Serve at room temperature.

Note: Adding ⅓ cup rum to the simmering syrup is a festive variation.

Black Walnut Clusters

Yield: 24 clusters

½ pound semisweet chocolate
1½ cups broken black walnut pieces

Melt the chocolate over hot (not boiling) water. Stir in the black walnut pieces. Drop by the tablespoon onto waxed paper. Let the clusters harden in a cool place, then remove them from the paper and store, covered, in a cool, dry place. Do not refrigerate or the chocolate might discolor. But whether you use black or common walnuts, the clusters are just too delicious to present long-term storage problems.

McIntosh Apples Call A Native Son Home

There are many reasons why people return to the places they were born. One of the most original I have heard is an apple. When I learned what kind of apple was involved, I understood. Here is how the Boston-born man explained it: "When I lived in California, it wasn't so much that I missed the changing of the seasons. No, the thing I longed for the most was a McIntosh apple."

I think about the young man when the second week of September brings the new crop of McIntoshes. The apples appear first at the farm stands in small white shopping bags. I never wait until I arrive home to enjoy the first McIntosh of the season. Rather, I take that first juice-bursting bite while sitting in my car. I bathe in the warmth of the September sun and enjoy the crisp, slightly tart taste. The juice runs down my fingers and I paw through the glove compartment for a tissue. I recall what the nuns at my parochial school said about improper girls who ate snacks in public view.

People who are fond of the tidier, sweeter Delicious apples don't understand the lure of the Macs — as the growers call them. I am married to a Delicious fancier. But then, while I am splashing my way through a lobster dripping with melted butter and lemon juice, he is content to spear fried clams with a fork.

The people who prefer Delicious apples outnumber the rest of us. Red and Yellow Delicious make up forty-eight percent of the eight billion pounds of apples grown annually in the United States. The other leading varieties are McIntosh, Granny Smith, and Rome Beauty.

Despite the phrase "as American as apple pie," the fruit is not native to North America. The first seeds were brought here by European settlers. The trees flourished in the rocky New England soil. Thanks to John Chapman, better known as Johnny Appleseed, orchards were planted in the early nineteenth century all over what was then the West: from Pennsylvania to Illinois.

There are ten thousand different varieties of apples grown worldwide. In the United States, we cultivate a mere seven thousand varieties, with wonderful names like Winesap, Wealthy, and Northern Spy.

If you enjoy vintage varieties, such as Sterling, Newton, and Roxbury Russett, you may be interested in the apple orchard museum in North Grafton, Massachusetts, where over one hundred old-fashioned varieties are nurtured.

The McIntosh apple grows best from Maine to the Champlain Valley. In New Hampshire, the Souhegan Valley is our thriving apple country. The Souhegans were one of New Hampshire's twelve tribes, and their name means "meadow people."

Wherever apples grow, the crop depends upon the whim of the weather months before harvest. One Christmas, for example, an unseasonable 25-degree-below-zero temperature frosted my house guests and at the same time pared the apple crop. Ten months later, the apple growers told me the crop was halved because that extreme cold spell arrived before the protective snow cover had blanketed the trees' roots.

How do you care for an apple? Listen to William Darrow, owner of Green Mountain Orchards in Putney, Vermont: "An apple is a living thing, like a vegetable, but people fail to remember that apples should always be refrigerated in a store or at home. An apple starts to run downhill like a head of lettuce if it is left on a kitchen counter."

Cooks who bake hundreds of pies for autumn church festivals use a device called a patent peeler. It reminds me of an old-fashioned clothes wringer. Occasionally, you can pick up an ancient cast-iron peeler at a flea market. There is a contemporary German model available in cook ware shops. The peeler skins an apple in ten seconds. You spear an apple on the blade and turn the handle.

Another useful tool, the cutter-corer, makes quick work of slicing apples for pies or snacks. This tool has blades arranged like spokes of a wheel, with the corer as the hub. The cutter-corer has no moving parts.

In America, the apple is the symbol of good things — apple-pie order, Mom and apple pie, and the apple of my eye. However, in Greek mythology, the fruit brought on a mighty crisis. When Eris, the goddess of discord, tossed a golden apple engraved "for the fairest" among the three other goddesses, the resulting scramble for the fruit set off the Trojan War.

Here are some peaceful ways to celebrate the fruit of autumn.

Chicken Roasted with Cider

Yield: 4 servings

3-pound whole broiler-fryer chicken
1 onion, diced
1 apple, cored, peeled, and chopped
¾ cup apple cider
Freshly ground black pepper
1 teaspoon dried rosemary

Preheat the oven to 350°F.

Rinse the chicken and pat dry. Place the chicken in a baking dish and fill the cavity with the onion and apple. Pour the cider over the chicken and sprinkle the pepper and rosemary over the whole bird.

Cover and bake for about 50 minutes, or until a leg can be easily moved at the joint. Remove the cover and let the chicken continue to brown for about 10 minutes. Serve with your favorite roast chicken fixings.

Apple Chutney

Yield: Approximately 10 half-pint jars

12 medium size ripe tomatoes, peeled
2 red hot peppers, finely chopped
2 green peppers, finely chopped
4 large tart apples, peeled, cored, and coarsely chopped
2½ cups firmly packed brown sugar
½ teaspoon ground cloves
1 cup chopped onion
1½ cups chopped celery
1½ cups cider vinegar
1 tablespoon dry mustard
1 tablespoon ground cinnamon

Combine all the ingredients in a large pot. Simmer for 30 to 45 minutes, or until the sauce appears quite thick. Watch carefully and stir as needed to prevent the chutney from scorching or sticking to the pan.

Pour into clean, hot half-pint canning jars. Seal. Process for 10 minutes in a boiling water bath. Cool and store in a cool, dry place. Or you can freeze the chutney in plastic containers.

This chutney goes nicely with roast chicken or pork, and with baked or broiled fish.

Danish Apple Cake

Yield: 8 servings

1 ½ cups unbleached all-purpose flour
1 cup sugar
½ cup butter, at room temperature
1 ½ teaspoons baking powder
1 egg
2 teaspoons vanilla extract
½ teaspoon ground cinnamon
4 large McIntosh apples
2 cups sour cream
2 egg yolks

A woman from Harrisville, New Hampshire, gave me this recipe. "It's a wonderful cake. It's really like a cheesecake, but much easier to make," she said.

* * *

Preheat the oven to 350°F. Position a rack in the center of the oven. Generously butter a 9-inch or 10-inch springform pan.

Combine the flour, ½ cup of the sugar, the butter, baking powder, egg, 1 teaspoon of the vanilla, and the cinnamon in a large bowl and mix thoroughly. Turn into the prepared pan.

Peel, core, and slice the apples. Layer on top of the batter.

Combine the sour cream, egg yolks, remaining ½ cup sugar, and remaining 1 teaspoon vanilla. Blend well. Pour over the apples. Bake for 1 hour, or until the edges of the custard are lightly browned.

Rich Pastry Dough

Yield: Dough for one 9-inch pie shell

1 cup unbleached all-purpose flour
1 tablespoon sugar
¼ cup unsalted butter, cut into 1-inch chunks
1 egg yolk
1 tablespoon vegetable oil
2 tablespoons ice water

Mix the flour, sugar, and butter in a food processor. Add the egg yolk and oil and process until mixed. With the machine still running, slowly add the ice water. Remove the dough and shape it into a ball. If the dough seems too sticky, lightly knead in a little more flour. Dust the ball of dough with flour and chill for at least 30 minutes. This dough can be frozen or stored in the refrigerator for several days. Then roll out to make a 9-inch pie shell.

Note: Butter is essential to this recipe. Do not substitute margarine.

Apple-Almond Tart

Yield: 8 servings

1 recipe Rich Pastry Dough (page 137)
3 pounds McIntosh apples
¼ cup butter
⅔ cup apple jelly
¼ cup sugar
1 teaspoon almond extract
½ cup coarsely chopped almonds

Prepare the pastry dough. While it is chilling, proceed with the filling. Preheat the oven to 350°F.

Peel, core, and quarter the apples. Melt the butter in a large skillet. Add the apples and cook over medium heat for 3 minutes, stirring occasionally. Add the jelly, sugar, and almond extract and mix thoroughly. Lower the heat and simmer for 5 minutes. Remove from the heat and cool the mixture to room temperature.

Meanwhile, roll out the crust on a floured board. Here is an easy way to transfer the pastry to the 9-inch pie pan: Place the pan upside down on the pastry and then invert the board. The pastry will drop into the pan. Any pastry sticking to the board can be loosened with a table knife. Trim the edges of the pastry.

Spoon the apples into the pastry shell and spread evenly. Bake for 40 minutes. Remove from the oven and sprinkle the almonds on top. Bake for 10 minutes more. Serve the tart at room temperature.

Chapter Eight

The Impossible Season

C ountry life provides plenty of leisurely moments to savor. But the season just before the snow flies is not one of them. The temperature keeps dropping and the snow is due any day; the chore list is impossibly long. We work against a backdrop of bare trees, biting wind, and gray skies, as anxious as squirrels to settle in our nests.

In the old days, people banked leaves against the foundations of their houses to keep out the cold. Now, we wrap our foundations with sheets of plastic to save fuel. People who postpone this chore until a windy November day often regret it.

The woods are full of hunters from the city, and that can be a hazard for us. We must collect and stack firewood on our weekends, and hunters must bag a deer on theirs. Thus, we try to gather our fuel supply before the hunters' siege begins.

Thanksgiving originated in New England and I am thankful that even today, the holiday retains the spirit intended by its founders. Now more than 350 years later, we still gather around the table, give thanks for our blessings, and toast the harvest.

Impossible Pies
For the Impossible Season

All it takes is one October rainstorm. You wake one morning and the foliage has disappeared. Just yesterday, the sugar maple and the dogwood flashed red and gold at us. Today, we crunch ankle deep in the leaves and stare at the naked branches.

That's when the impossible season begins for northern New Englanders — the foot-and-hand-race to get everything done before a foot of snow covers the dooryard.

Of course, thanks to the infinite variety of New England weather, there have been years when we missed out on the impossible season altogether. For example, in 1979, an October 10 snowstorm added a new dimension to the splendors of the foliage. One frugal and philosophical innkeeper pointed out that his guests got two New Hampshire seasons for the price of one.

But that snowstorm was a rarity. Most years we have a few weeks to finish our wintering-in chores before the first storm covers the earth and makes those chores very difficult or impossible.

Firewood must be hauled out of the woods, cut, and stacked. Scavenger hunts are organized to find matching boots and mittens, windshield scrapers, thermal underwear, and caulking guns.

Cabinetmaker Terry Cox, who lives in nearby Westmoreland, and who would rather carve rosewood and mahogany than stack and split firewood, tells me this season always reminds him of his brother who lives in San Diego, California. "I think about him a lot these October weekends, floating in his condominium pool, drinking tequila sunrises," the cabinetmaker says.

Our gardens must be put to bed with a blanket of winter rye. I fill the flowerpots with spring bulbs and stash them in the cellar. When I bring them upstairs next January, the unfolding crocuses and tulips will add immeasurably to my midwinter mental health.

As we race about our chores, we keep an eye on the pewter sky. Nature tightens up the game by decreasing the amount of light at each end of the day.

Thank goodness the birds harvest the overabundance of sunflower seeds. And the wind does a better job of raking all those leaves than I possibly could.

That's why in this season I bless the anonymous inventor of the impossible pies. The formula is simple: All you do is pour a batter over a pie plate lined with such ingredients as shredded cheese, chopped vegetables, or fruit. As the impossible pie bakes, it makes its own crust. These pies have other names, such as can't-believe-it quiche, surprise pie, no-crust pie, and bottomless pie.

Discovering impossible pies is like learning new words — suddenly they appear in every cookbook you read. Many of the recipes call for biscuit mix. I've learned you can substitute flour for the mix if you add a bit of baking powder. If the recipe calls for 1 cup of biscuit mix, use 1 cup of unbleached all-purpose flour and 1 teaspoon of baking powder.

The following are impossible pies that are especially good in this season.

Marjorie's Impossible Swedish Apple Pie

Yield: 6 servings

6 to 8 apples, peeled, cored, and sliced
1 tablespoon plus 1 cup sugar
1 teaspoon ground cinnamon
1 cup unbleached all-purpose flour
1 egg, beaten
¾ cup margarine, melted

Preheat the oven to 350°F.

Fill a well-greased 9-inch pie plate three-quarters full with sliced apples. Sprinkle with 1 tablespoon sugar and the cinnamon.

Stir together the remaining 1 cup sugar and the flour. Add the egg and margarine and stir until blended. The mixture will be thick.

Spread the mixture over the apples. Bake for 30 minutes; then increase the temperature to 400° and bake for 15 minutes. Serve either warm or cold.

ADD SOME ALMOND EXTRACT

Impossible Cranberry Pie

Yield: 6 servings

2 cups cranberries
1⅓ cups sugar
½ cup walnuts, coarsely chopped
2 tablespoons orange juice
2 eggs
¾ cup butter, melted
1 cup unbleached all-purpose flour

Preheat the oven to 325°F.

Put the cranberries in a well-greased 10-inch pie plate. Sprinkle with ⅓ cup of the sugar, the walnuts, and orange juice.

If you have a blender or a food processor, combine the eggs, the remaining 1 cup sugar, the butter, and the flour in the machine and whirl at high speed for 15 seconds, or until just smooth.

Otherwise, beat the eggs in a large bowl. Then beat in the remaining 1 cup sugar and the butter. Stir in the flour.

Spread the batter over the berry mixture. Bake for 1 hour, or until the crust is golden. Serve either warm or cold.

End-of-the-Garden Impossible Pie

Yield: 6 servings

½ green pepper, chopped
1½ cups chopped zucchini
1 cup chopped tomato
½ cup chopped onion
⅓ cup grated cheddar cheese
1 cup milk
½ cup unbleached all-purpose flour
2 eggs
½ teaspoon salt
½ teaspoon dried basil
½ teaspoon dried oregano

Preheat the oven to 400°F.

Layer the pepper, zucchini, tomato, and onion in a well-greased 9-inch pie plate. Sprinkle with the cheese.

If you have a blender or a food processor, combine the milk, flour, eggs, salt, basil, and oregano in the machine and whirl at high speed for 15 seconds, or until just smooth.

Otherwise, beat the eggs in a large bowl. Then beat in remaining ingredients.

Pour the mixture over the vegetables. Bake for about 30 minutes, or until a knife inserted about 1 inch from the center comes out clean. Let the pie stand for 5 minutes before slicing.

Note: If fresh basil and oregano are available, I prefer to use 1 teaspoon of each.

Impossible Quiche

Yield: 6 servings

½ pound (about 12 slices) bacon
½ cup finely chopped onion
1 cup grated Swiss cheese
2 cups milk
½ cup unbleached all-purpose flour
½ teaspoon baking powder
4 eggs
¼ teaspoon salt
½ teaspoon black pepper
¼ teaspoon Tabasco sauce (optional)

Preheat the oven to 350°F.

Cook the bacon until crisp in a medium-size skillet. Or bake the bacon in an aluminum-foil-lined baking pan for about 10 minutes at 400°. Drain the bacon on paper towels. Cool and crumble.

Place the bacon and onion in a well-greased 9-inch pie plate. Sprinkle with the cheese.

If you have a blender or a food processor, combine the milk, flour, baking powder, eggs, salt, pepper, and Tabasco (if desired) in the machine and whirl at high speed for 15 seconds, or until just smooth.

Otherwise, beat the eggs in a large bowl. Then beat in the remaining ingredients.

Pour the mixture over the ingredients in the pie plate. Bake for 50 to 55 minutes, or until a knife inserted about 1 inch from the center comes out clean. Let stand for 5 minutes before slicing.

Put pieces of ham (cooked) or turkey etc.

Bear Meat Recipes
For the Game Cook

Cooking bear has not been one of my specialties. However, when it comes to trying new food, I'm game.

The first step is tracking down a source of the meat. I have since discovered it may be simpler to hunt and shoot a bear or even buy an entire bear from a successful hunter than it is to buy a pound of the flesh. A conservation officer told me a New Hampshire hunter may sell the one bear he is allowed to bag each year. Thus, New Hampshire residents often sell their bear kill to less-skilled hunters from the big cities. All I needed was a couple of pounds. The conservation officer explained that grocers don't bother selling bear because a few steaks aren't worth the tangle of multi-agency red tape.

I asked around and learned that Arthur Bowers of the nearby town of Troy, New Hampshire, had bagged a bear on Labor Day weekend in the White Mountains. It was his third bear in as many years. Naturally, he refused to disclose exactly where he found his bear.

Mr. Bowers also refused to take any money for his bear meat. "It's good publicity for me," he chuckled. He's been selling hunting equipment, such as bows, arrows, and guns, for years. Later, I realized he really didn't care about any publicity for his business, but like all hunters and fishers, he wanted the world to know about the one that did not get away.

In any case, Mr. Bowers gave me a couple of bear steaks and two pounds of ground bear for my project.

Mr. Bowers warned that bear meat must be handled properly from the beginning. "Years ago, I learned a secret from a Maine Indian guide. He told me to dress it off (eviscerate and bleed the game) right away and cool it in a brook. These days, I dress the bear right away and stow it in a freezer up north until I am ready to drive home."

The custom of draping a bear on the front of a car to display it only ruins good bear meat, Mr. Bowers said.

He also suggested removing all the fat before cooking the meat, because he thinks bear fat adds nothing to the taste.

Now, where does one find a recipe for cooking bear? The index in most cookbooks merely reads, "beans, Béarnaise, béchamel."

However, I persisted and discovered two principles of bear cooking recommended by New Hampshire and Maine cooperative extension workers.

First, handle bear as you do pork. Bear, like pork, may contain a parasite that causes trichinosis. The disease is serious and attacks the muscular system. However, proper cooking destroys the parasite. That means cooking the bear to an internal temperature of at least 137°F. To be perfectly safe, use a meat thermometer and cook a bear roast until the internal temperature is 170°. Further, never taste raw bear meat. After handling the meat, wash everything it touched — hands, meat grinders, cutting boards — with hot water and detergent.

Second, it is a good idea to marinate bear steaks and loins before cooking. Marinating the meat for eight to twenty-four hours tenderizes it and lessens the strong, gamy taste.

I prepared the bear steaks first, marinating them in vinegar, oil, and mixed pickling spices. Then I covered the steaks with tomatoes and peppers and braised them Swiss style. The result was a tender, beeflike meat. Strong-tasting, gamy, but good. The flavor was even better the next day, when I reheated and served samples of the leftovers to a pair of curious carpenters who were working on my house.

The next project was the bear loaf. I made a standard meat loaf and adapted it slightly for the bear. The loaf tasted better than the steaks. Perhaps my palate was learning.

Some friends who turned down the bear steaks accepted the bear loaf. The loaf-eaters agreed that bear meat is rich and hearty. One thin slice will do.

What does one drink with bear meat? It depends on how it is prepared. My choices would be a good, strong beer or a hearty, dry red wine, such as a Burgundy or Chianti.

Swiss Bear
Yield: 6 servings

1 can (16 ounces) plum tomatoes
2 pounds bear steaks, cut into serving-size pieces
2 tablespoons white distilled vinegar
2 tablespoons vegetable oil
1 tablespoon mixed pickling spices
½ teaspoon salt
1 green pepper, sliced into ½-inch rings
12 fresh mushrooms
2 medium-size onions, sliced

Drain the liquid from the tomatoes. Set the tomatoes aside. Place the bear steaks in a shallow, nonmetallic dish. Mix together the vinegar, oil, tomato liquid, pickling spices, and salt. Pour over the steaks. Cover and refrigerate overnight.

Place the steaks in a baking dish. Add the tomatoes, pepper, mushrooms, and onions. Pour the marinade over all. Cover and bake at 350°F. for 1½ hours, or until tender.

Note: Instead of bear, you can use 2 pounds beef round steak or venison steak.

Venison or Elk Sauerbraten

Yield: 6 servings

2 cups white distilled vinegar
2 cups water
2 tablespoons pure maple syrup or sugar
12 whole cloves
4 bay leaves
1 teaspoon mustard seeds
2 teaspoons salt (optional)
Freshly ground black pepper
3-pound piece venison or elk
3 onions, sliced
3 carrots, sliced
⅓ cup gingersnap crumbs
2 cups water
⅓ cup sour cream

This game version of sauerbraten needs a few days' lead time for marinating. It goes nicely with buttered noodles and a simple green salad.

* * *

In a large bowl or crock, combine the vinegar, water, maple syrup, and seasonings. Add the meat and store in the refrigerator for 2 to 4 days, turning the meat once a day.

When you are ready to cook, remove the meat and strain the marinade. Place the meat in a heavy pot with 1 cup of the marinade. Add the vegetables; bring to a boil. Lower the heat and simmer, covered, for 3 to 4 hours, until tender.

Remove the meat to a warm platter. Stir the gingersnap crumbs and the water into the mixture remaining in the pot. Cook until the gravy is slightly thickened. Stir in the sour cream. Heat, but do not boil.

Slice the meat into ½-inch-thick slices and set them, overlapping, on a warm serving platter. Put the gravy in a warmed gravy boat and serve on the side.

Bear Loaf

Yield: 4 servings

3½ tablespoons butter
1 cup minced onion
1 pound lean ground
  bear meat
1 egg, beaten
½ teaspoon dried
  thyme
½ teaspoon dried
  basil
½ teaspoon dried
  marjoram
½ teaspoon dried sage
Dash freshly ground
  black pepper
¼ cup dry bread
  crumbs
¼ cup dry white wine
1 cup sliced fresh
  mushrooms

Melt 2 tablespoons of the butter in a frying pan. Add the onion and sauté until soft. Combine the onion, meat, egg, herbs, pepper, bread crumbs, and wine.

In a shallow baking pan, shape the meat mixture into a loaf. Place in a 325°F. oven and bake for 1 hour. Transfer to a heated serving platter and keep warm.

Melt the remaining 1½ tablespoons butter in a frying pan. Add the mushrooms and sauté until golden brown. Surround the meat loaf with the mushrooms and serve.

Note: If you can't bag a bear, use ground beef or ground venison instead.

Boiled Dinner
And Red Flannel Hash

When the November wind sweeps up the leaves and makes our house creak with its great age, the time has come for a New England boiled dinner. The Yankee who invented this dish thoughtfully provided the next day's menu, too. In New England, one day's boiled dinner yields the next day's red flannel hash.

I rediscovered this American version of pot au feu when a fierce ice storm disconnected our electric power for three days. At first, reading by kerosene lamp and cuddling in down sleeping bags was amusing. Not to mention feeling righteous about surviving on cheese, crackers, and orange juice. But soon we hungered for hot food and drink. We drove down to the valley, where seven hundred feet below our ice-coated hill it had been raining, but the electric current still flowed. We waded across the parking lot toward the brightly lit diner. Steam curtained the large windows. Inside, a utility repair crew fueled up on fried clams and hot turkey sandwiches.

The night's special was New England boiled dinner, which I ordered because I was too cold and weary to read a menu. Minutes later, a platter of pink meat surrounded by carrots, turnips, and a wedge of cabbage was set before me. The steaming broth warmed my face and psyche the way a sauna warms the bones, and I knew I could endure one more night in that dark, chilly house.

Boiled dinner was called corned beef and cabbage in the Irish neighborhood where I grew up; and if you had it for dinner, you didn't brag about it to the other children. This was America in the 1950s, and the message was to forget your origins and aim for the T-bone steak with a baked potato wrapped in aluminum foil.

There was even a comic strip that kept corned beef and cabbage in its place. It featured Jiggs, a self-made rich man, who sneaked out of the mansion for a bit of the humble dish at Dinty Moore's Tavern. His wife, the upwardly mobile, butler-attended Maggie, always found out and greeted her husband with a swing of the rolling pin as he walked in the door.

Mention boiled dinner to New Englanders and they will respond in one of two ways. They will tell you they love the dish and that their grandmother's version can be traced back to colonial times — perhaps even to the slab of salted beef stashed in the hold of the *Mayflower*. Or, a Yankee will say he doesn't like the stuff, but the people who used to live in the Irish part of town sure did eat a lot of it.

An eighty-one-year-old neighbor told me his father operated a meat wagon in a nearby town during the 1880s. The butcher-on-wheels loaded his wagon with sides of meat and cut his customers' meat to order at each stop. When he arrived in the Irish neighborhood, he quickly sold out his supply of brisket, which was used for corned beef dinners.

When I advertised for information leading to the origins of the boiled dinner, one person not only sent me her grandmother's recipe for the dish but also the recipe for corning the beef. "After reading Julia Child's recipe, we believe my grandmother's might be the more traditional New England type."

Rosemary Bernheimer of Keene, New Hampshire, wrote, "The beef was corned for winter use as most butchering was done in the fall." She added that her mother didn't stop at adding cabbage. "Most root cellar or 'keeping' vegetables were also added — carrots, potatoes, turnips, and parsnips. She also preferred using the round instead of the brisket they now use. She thought the brisket was too fatty. Since pork was less expensive than beef, sometimes we used smoked shoulder and ham to replace the beef." The writer said that the boiled dinner was a popular dish as far back as fifty-five years ago.

Traditionally, politicians organize corned beef and cabbage dinners to celebrate St. Patrick's Day and woo the voters from the Irish wards in such places as South Boston and South Buffalo. Wouldn't the pols be surprised to learn about the luncheon menu planned by the ultimate Republican for his inauguration day? President Abraham Lincoln invited his guests to the Willard Hotel for mock turtle soup, corned beef and cabbage, parsley potatoes, and blackberry pie, according to the 1964 edition of *The American Heritage Cookbook.*

The corning of beef, it turns out, has nothing to do with corn. It refers to preserving the meat by coating it with coarse grains of salt rather than pickling it in brine. Even so, both methods were used to produce the meat for boiled dinner.

If you prefer to pass the salt because you are concerned about sodium intake, consider substituting fresh beef for the corned meat. And remember, boiled dinner is not boiled at all; it is simmered.

If red flannel hash is not your dish, use the leftover meat for corned beef on rye sandwiches.

New Englanders often cooked their dessert in the same pot as the boiled dinner. In an old cookbook from Swanzey, New Hampshire, Winifred Goodell's Bag Pudding calls for buttermilk, eggs, flour, raisins, butter, and cornmeal. The dough is placed in a cloth bag and boiled for 1½ hours with the beef and cabbage. The pudding is served with sweetened, nutmeg-flavored cream. In some parts of the United States, bag pudding is called Son of a Gun in a Sack.

And I had been under the impression that boil-in-a-bag dishes were invented by space-age technology.

Red Flannel Hash

Yield: 6 servings

1½ cups chopped cooked corned beef
1½ cups chopped cooked beets
3 cups chopped cooked potatoes
½ cup chopped onion
1 garlic clove, minced
½ teaspoon dry mustard
1 grind fresh black pepper
½ cup light cream
Salt
¼ cup fat, preferably bacon drippings
6 eggs (optional)
Chopped fresh parsley, for garnish

Combine the corned beef, beets, potatoes, onion, garlic, mustard, pepper, and cream in a bowl. Toss lightly. Add salt to taste.

Melt the fat in a 9-inch or 10-inch frying pan and add the corned beef mixture. Press down the hash until the bottom of the pan is evenly covered. Cook, uncovered, over moderate heat for 25 to 30 minutes, or until the bottom is browned.

Or bake the hash for 45 minutes at 350°F. in a well-greased 9-inch square pan.

To serve with eggs, poach the eggs and place 1 egg on top of each serving. Garnish with fresh parsley.

Corned Beef, Kosher Style

Yield: 8 to 10 servings

1 cup salt
2 quarts water
2 tablespoons sugar
2 garlic cloves
1 teaspoon paprika
1 tablespoon mixed
  pickling spices
¼ teaspoon saltpeter
5 pounds beef brisket
  or rump
Water
4 bay leaves
1 teaspoon whole
  cloves
1 medium-size onion,
  sliced

Combine the salt, water, sugar, garlic, paprika, and pickling spices in a large pot. Bring to a boil and simmer gently for 15 minutes. Cool to warm and stir in the saltpeter. Pour the liquid into a stone or glass crock. Add the meat, cover with a plate, and weight with a stone. Let stand for 3 weeks in a cool place, turning occasionally.

To cook the corned beef, rinse to draw off the extra salt. Place the meat in a large pot and add water just to cover the meat. Add the bay leaves, cloves, and onion. Bring to a boil. Lower the heat and simmer for 3 to 4 hours until the meat is fork-tender.

Remove the meat from the liquid, slice, and serve warm. Accompaniments can include sour cream flavored with prepared mustard and grated horseradish, braised cabbage, and boiled potatoes.

This corned beef also can be served warm or cold in sandwiches such as the New York Reuben, which consists of corned beef, Swiss cheese, and sauerkraut on rye bread.

Or use the corned brisket for the New England Boiled Dinner (page 150).

Note: Saltpeter is one of the nitrates and you may prefer to omit it. Traditionally, it is added to corned beef to intensify the meat's pinkness.

New England Boiled Dinner

Yield: 6 to 8 servings

4-pound to 5-pound corned brisket of beef
Cold water
1 teaspoon dried basil
½ teaspoon dried thyme
1 bay leaf
8 carrots, peeled
4 parsnips, peeled
8 potatoes, peeled
6 turnips, peeled and cut into sixths
1 small head green cabbage, cut into sixths

Cover the beef with cold water and let stand for 30 minutes to draw out excess salt. Remove the beef and discard the water. Place the beef in a large pot and cover with fresh cold water. Add the basil, thyme, and bay leaf. Bring to a boil and reduce the heat to a simmer. Skim the fat from the surface as necessary. Cook gently for 3 to 4 hours until the beef is fork-tender.

About 30 minutes before serving, add all the vegetables, except the cabbage. Add the cabbage 15 to 20 minutes before serving. Turn up the heat when adding the vegetables so that the broth continues to bubble. Turn the heat down again when the simmering point is reached.

To serve, place the beef on a large platter and surround with vegetables.

Note: Variations include using a plain brisket of beef, if a corned brisket is too salty for your taste. Or consider varying the flavor by adding a cup of apple cider to the beef and water when beginning to cook.

Traditional accompaniments to a boiled dinner are pickled beets, mustard pickles, and corn bread.

Miniature Reuben Sandwiches   *Yield: 50 sandwiches*

Good mustard
Mayonnaise
1 loaf party rye bread
**1 pound good corned
  beef, thinly sliced**
**1 package or can (1
  pound) sauerkraut**
**½ pound Swiss
  cheese, thinly sliced**

The invitation to the housewarming party asked the guests to bring an hors d'oeuvre. The response was impressive — pâté, baguette, smoked oyster spread, hot crab dip. But I stayed close to a plate of Gail Talbot's miniature Reuben sandwiches. The house that was warmed has since been sold and warmed again. But those little Reubens continue to haunt my hungry moments.

Gail describes herself as a "dump cook" — one who never writes down a recipe. Here is her best guess for her formula. "Make a billion, as they are wonderfully popular. When we are making a lot, we work on an assembly line. It's fun!" Gail says.

* * *

At least 2 hours before serving, spread the mustard and mayonnaise on the bread. Then add a layer of corned beef and a layer of sauerkraut. Top with the cheese. When ready to serve, broil open-faced until the cheese is bubbly, 2 to 3 minutes. Serve at once.

Thanksgiving:
A Simple New England Feast

Thanksgiving is a favorite holiday of mine. I savor its simplicity. We give thanks and celebrate our blessings with good company and good food. Even as I assemble a Thanksgiving dinner, I am reminded of my blessings at every turn: my mother's china, my mother-in-law's goblets, a great-aunt's turkey platter, and a friend's family recipe for cornbread sausage stuffing.

I think about my first Thanksgiving in New Hampshire. The day was warm and my husband's children played touch football on the lawn. Edward asked them what they thought about him marrying me. The girls, who were then teen-agers, giggled and said, "Oh, Dad, we think you should marry Julie." My predecessor. I knew then that our family — prefab though it may be — was blessed with a sense of humor.

I remember another Thanksgiving when Edward was very sick and his illness was just one more trial in a year that had been difficult for each of us. There didn't seem to be much point in counting blessings or roasting chestnuts. But I decided to prepare a scaled-down turkey dinner for just the two of us.

As I was about to slice and serve an apple cheesecake for dessert, our new kitten plunged into the middle of the cake to grab a grape from the garnish. We gave thanks for the unexpected laugh over the mangled dessert and even more thanks that a finicky guest had not witnessed the event.

I think about Thanksgivings as recent as five years ago when my sister Roberta and I would stir squash and pinch turkey thighs for doneness, while our husbands sat in the living room working out the world's problems over glasses of wine. These days, we all stir and sip and chat over the hot stove. It was in one of these kitchen-cabinet sessions that my brother-in-law Tom confided he really didn't like pumpkin pie, and we have had chocolate endings for Thanksgivings ever since.

I am thankful a determined daughter of New Hampshire decided that a country as rich as the United States ought to give thanks as a nation once a year. Sarah Josepha Hale began her campaign in 1827; President Lincoln finally proclaimed Thanksgiving a national holiday in 1863.

Mrs. Hale was born in Newport, New Hampshire. As a young widow with a brood to support, she moved to Boston and later to Philadelphia to earn a living. She became the first woman editor in the United States, encouraged women writers and artists, and fought for the education and employment of women. As editor of *Godey's Lady's Book,* she reached thousands of readers, and she urged them to "make America recognized in every quarter of the world for its gratitude for its blessings."

It may surprise you that several modern Thanksgiving activities go back two or three centuries. When you go out for your annual cranberry five-mile run, remember that Chief Massasoit and his 90 braves challenged the Plymouth settlers to running games back at Thanksgiving 1621. When you take a chance on a turkey raffle, be aware that the custom of raffling off a bird on Thanksgiving Eve was already a popular tradition in the early nineteenth century. We do know the first Thanksgiving menu included venison, wild turkey, and corn. The feast also may have included pumpkin, squash, and cranberries. The turkey, cranberries, and pumpkin pie are still on the menu for most Americans. But the rest of the menu reflects regional tastes.

I, for one, never encountered a creamed onion before I moved to New England. But creamed onions are a typical item on the Yankee Thanksgiving menu along with butternut squash flavored with maple syrup, oyster and sausage or giblet stuffing, fresh cranberry-orange relish, mashed potatoes, yams, and pumpkin pie or Indian pudding. Recent additions to the traditional fare are fruit breads, such as pumpkin or cranberry-walnut.

The following are favorite Thanksgiving dishes among northern New Englanders.

You may or may not be thankful I was unable to track down a recipe for creamed onions.

Corn Bread Sausage Stuffing

Yield: Enough stuffing for a 16-pound to 20-pound turkey

¼ cup butter
1 cup chopped onion
2 pounds bulk sausage
8 cups soft stale corn bread crumbs
½ teaspoon black pepper
1 teaspoon dried thyme
½ cup chopped fresh parsley
1 teaspoon dried sage
½ teaspoon salt
Chicken broth (optional)

Melt the butter in a large skillet. Add the onion and cook until translucent. Pour into a large bowl. Place the sausage meat in the skillet and cook, breaking it up with a fork.

Pour off the fat from the cooked sausage, reserving about 1 tablespoon. Add the 1 tablespoon fat to the onion in the bowl. Add the sausage, bread crumbs, pepper, thyme, parsley, sage, and salt. Toss lightly. If you desire a moister stuffing, add a bit of chicken broth.

Note: Ordinary bread crumbs can be substituted for the corn bread. I usually make a 9-inch square loaf of corn bread to use for the crumbs. It is extra work, but I think the taste of the sausage and the corn bread is worth the trouble.

Indian Pudding

Yield: 6 servings

2 eggs, beaten
¼ cup sugar
½ cup molasses
1 tablespooon butter, softened
1 teaspoon ground cinnamon
½ teaspoon ground ginger
¼ teaspoon ground nutmeg
3 cups milk
¼ cup cornmeal
½ cup cold water
½ teaspoon salt
½ cup raisins
1 pint (2 cups) light cream

Indian pudding is so named because the recipe calls for cornmeal, which the colonists regarded as Indian flour. The pudding tastes best when served hot, swimming in light cream.

* * *

Preheat the oven to 350°F.

Mix together the eggs, sugar, molasses, butter, and spices. Set aside.

Scald the milk in the top of a double boiler. Mix the cornmeal, water, and salt in a small bowl. Stir into the scalded milk. Cook and stir over boiling water for about 10 minutes.

Remove from the heat and stir in the raisins and butter-spice mixture.

Pour into a buttered 1½-quart baking dish or 9-inch square pan and set the baking dish into a pan of water. Bake for 1 hour, or until a knife inserted 1 inch from the center comes out clean. Spoon into serving dishes, pour on the cream, and serve.

Elma Cranberry Salad

Yield: 9 servings

1 package (6 ounces)
  raspberry or lemon
  gelatin
3 cups boiling water
½ cup sugar
1 tablespoon lemon
  juice
1 can (8 ounces)
  unsweetened
  crushed pineapple
1 medium-size orange
2 cups fresh
  cranberries
½ cup chopped celery
½ cup chopped
  walnuts

Until I was a college senior, a cranberry was a cylinder of jelly that slipped out of a can and onto a plate for Thanksgiving dinner. I discovered fresh cranberry salad when I was shipped off to Elma, New York, for a semester to learn about farm life. My friend Margaret and I boarded on a farm where several generations of a family lived. Although we home economics students were astounded by the rather bizarre conduct at the evening meal, we enjoyed generous helpings of excellent food. Among the platters was this cranberry salad prepared in a star-shaped mold.

* * *

Dissolve the gelatin in the boiling water. Stir in the sugar, lemon juice, and undrained pineapple. Chill until partially set.

Quarter and seed the orange but do not peel. Put the cranberries and orange through a food chopper. Stir into the gelatin mixture along with the celery and walnuts. Turn into a 2½-quart mold or a 9-inch square pan. Refrigerate until set, about 4 hours. Unmold and serve.

Brandied Pumpkin Pie

Yield: 6 servings

1 unbaked 9-inch pie
  shell
2 cups cooked
  pumpkin purée
⅔ cup firmly packed
  brown sugar
2 teaspoons ground
  cinnamon
½ teaspoon ground
  ginger
⅛ teaspoon ground
  cloves
¾ cup milk
2 eggs, beaten
1 cup heavy cream
¼ cup brandy
Whipped cream
  (optional)

Prepare the pie shell and refrigerate while assembling the filling. Preheat the oven to 450°F.

Combine the pumpkin, brown sugar, and spices in a large bowl. Beat in the milk, eggs, cream, and brandy.

Pour the pumpkin mixture into the pie shell and bake for 15 minutes. Reduce the heat to 350° and bake for about 45 minutes longer, or until a knife blade inserted about 1 inch from the center comes out clean. Cool before serving. Top with whipped cream, if desired.

Chapter Nine

An Upcountry Christmas

C hristmas is just the excuse I need to pursue the pleasures of baking. I don't get into a frenzy about it. Any time it stops being fun, I quit. Christmas baking can start early in November because the season's specialties, such as fruitcake and plum pudding, need to age. Some years, I don't have time to bake anything until the weekend before Christmas.

Most of the things I make during this season are gifts. A dozen homemade cookies is one way to say thanks or "I like you" without overwhelming or obligating someone.

I also enjoy decorating or wrapping a gift from the kitchen. I am not talking about constructing a Victorian gingerbread mansion roofed with candy corn shingles. Topping a jar of mustard pickles with a bonnet of red calico is more my style.

Christmas is also a good time to introduce children to the sweetness of giving something they made themselves. Some evening, shut off the television or the video games and let the children make the cookies or wrap the fudge. Such memories are guaranteed to outlive those of any battery-powered toy.

Holiday Baking: Enjoy It, Avoid It, Or Wrap It Up for Gifts

If you enjoy baking as I do, the Christmas season brings a double pleasure: making good things and giving a bit of yourself to others.

For eleven months of the year, we count pennies, minutes, and calories. But every December, I, for one, enjoy buying the butter, the mincemeat, the cardamom pods, and the almonds by the pound.

I savor the act of baking as much as the results. There must be time to work slowly and to enjoy the shapes of the cookie cutters — the angel, the Santa, and the Christmas tree.

Not everyone has the time or the desire to make holiday goodies. In New England you can shop the church bazaars instead. In our town, eight churches hold their Christmas fairs on the first Saturday in December. Each of the committees works for months to come up with a fresh theme for their bazaar. No matter what they call it — Babes in Toyland, the Nutcracker Sweet, or Christmas in the Canary Islands — we all know the Methodists still make the best peanut butter fudge; the Episcopalians, the finest shortbread; the Congregationalists, the best-buy shopper's lunch; and the Catholics, the tastiest bourbon balls.

If you are too busy to shop for Christmas breads and desserts, consider delegating the chore to someone who likes to cook and can use extra cash. One busy woman makes a deal with her baby sitter. "At Thanksgiving, we sit down and figure out what I will need for gifts and entertaining. I get wonderful cookies and cakes, which Linda makes from her mother's Swedish recipes. It takes a lot of pressure off me," she explained.

Whenever I wrap cookies, I think of my friend Margaret McMahon Horrigan. In college, she always added a classy touch to her home economics projects. If our assignment in tailoring class was making a suit, Margaret also made a divine blouse. She was the one who thought about centerpieces when we invited the faculty to lunch in the sterile food lab. We teased her about the extras because we were too young to appreciate what those touches meant to her and the people who were mature enough to enjoy them.

At Christmas, Margaret loved to try new cookies. She placed some of each variety on a sturdy plate, covered the plate with plastic wrap, and added a bright satin bow. The lucky people on her list began thinking about chocolate mint cookies around the first of December.

Another friend gives pickles, preserves, and jams for Christmas. Instead of wrapping a jar in paper — which is hard to do — she cuts a circle of gingham or calico one inch larger than the top of the jar. She places the fabric on the jar's top and fastens it with a belt of ribbon or yarn. The gift looks as if it came off the shelf at Fortum & Mason and the raspberry jam or mustard pickles are appealingly visible. For a special gift, she packs a picnic hamper with fruit butters, jellies, and relishes plus a bottle or two of her homemade lemon balm or raspberry liqueur.

I like to include the recipe with any gift of food. Sometimes I package a loaf of pumpkin bread with a breadboard or place a batch of cookies in a basket lined with a checked napkin.

During the rest of the year, you can often find old-fashioned canning or apothecary jars at flea markets or rummage sales. Wash the jars and use them to hold dry mixtures, such as tea, granola, snacks, or seasoned rice.

For gift tags, take a tip from a frugal Yankee: Cut them from last year's Christmas cards; use a paper punch to make a hole for inserting yarn or cord.

One of my favorite holiday cookies is flavored with anise. My earliest memory of any Christmas sweet was an anise-scented square thick with frosting so sweet it stung the teeth. These days, I skip the thick pink frosting, but I still love the little cakes touched with that wonderful spice.

Anise happens to be one of the oldest-known aromatic seeds. In Biblical times, taxes were paid in anise seeds. Imagine dragging a sack of anise seeds to the town clerk's office. Or quibbling with the selectmen about the assessed value of your house in anise seeds.

In Europe, a wedding cake must include anise seeds to ensure good luck.

I don't know whether my good fortune is due to all the cookies I have eaten that were lush with the scent of anise. But all of the cookies here have brought me that compliment of compliments: "Please write down that recipe for me."

Spice-Almond Buttons
Yield: 12 dozen cookies

2¼ cups sifted unbleached all-purpose flour
1 tablespoon powdered instant coffee
1 teaspoon baking powder
1 teaspoon pumpkin pie spice
½ teaspoon salt
½ cup margarine
⅓ cup firmly packed brown sugar
1 egg
½ cup molasses
1 cup finely chopped unblanched almonds

Sift together the flour, coffee, baking powder, pie spice, and salt.

Cream the margarine with the brown sugar until light. Beat in the egg and molasses. Stir in the flour mixture, half at a time, to make a soft dough. Chill overnight.

Preheat the oven to 350°F.

Roll the dough, ½ teaspoon at a time, into marble-size balls. Roll in the almonds. Place the balls 1 inch apart on a lightly greased baking sheet. Flatten to ¼ inch thickness with the bottom of a glass.

Bake for 10 minutes. Remove immediately from the baking sheet and cool on a wire rack.

Margaret's Anise Cookies

Yield: Approximately 3½ dozen cookies

2 eggs, at room
   temperature
¾ cup sugar
½ teaspoon anise
   extract
1½ cups unbleached
   all-purpose flour
¼ teaspoon baking
   powder

Christmas is the perfect season for making these cookies because the house is cool and dry. That's the atmosphere you need to dry the cookies for 12 hours before baking.

* * *

With an electric mixer, beat the eggs. Gradually add in the sugar and beat the mixture until very thick and pale yellow. Beat in the anise extract.

Sift the flour and baking powder together. Gently fold the flour into the egg mixture, one-third at a time. Drop the dough by the teaspoon onto greased cookie sheets about 1½ inches apart.

Let the cookies stand, uncovered, overnight at room temperature. Do not refrigerate. Bake on the middle rack of a preheated 350°F. oven for 5 to 6 minutes, or until pale gold.

Remove from the sheet and cool on a rack. Store in an airtight container.

Mona Flagg's Fruitcake

Yield: One 10-inch cake

2 cups dark raisins
2 cups golden raisins
1 cup pitted dates,
  chopped
½ cup candied
  cherries
⅔ cup candied
  pineapple
⅓ cup candied orange
  or lemon rind
1 cup chopped
  walnuts
2 cups port wine
1 cup butter, softened
1 cup sugar
1 tablespoon vanilla
  extract
6 eggs
5 cups graham
  cracker crumbs
Wine

Mona's spirited fruitcake brings a bit of cheer to Christmas-time coffee breaks. Be sure to begin making this cake 1 month before you plan to serve it.

* * *

In a large bowl, mix all the fruits, nuts, and 1 cup of the wine. Let stand for several days. (Try not to taste it all the time, as it is very good and very hard to leave alone.) Check occasionally and add additional wine as the fruit absorbs it.

When you are ready to bake, preheat the oven to 250°F.

Cream the butter, sugar, and vanilla. Beat in the eggs, 2 at a time. Beat in the cracker crumbs. Mix in the fruit and any remaining wine from the original 2 cups.

Grease a 10-inch tube pan. Line with waxed paper. Pour in the batter and bake for 3½ to 4 hours. Cool the cake in the pan. Then remove from the pan and peel off the paper.

Wrap the cake in cheesecloth and sprinkle with wine. Wrap in aluminum foil and store in a cool place. Sprinkle with wine once a week until you are ready to serve the cake.

Kriss Kringle Canes

Yield: 5 dozen cookies

2¾ cups unbleached
all-purpose flour
3 teaspoons baking
powder
1 teaspoon salt
¾ teaspoon ground
cinnamon
⅛ teaspoon ground
nutmeg
½ cup margarine
1½ cups sugar
1 egg
1 teaspoon grated
lemon rind
1 teaspoon vanilla
extract
½ cup milk
Red food coloring

Preheat the oven to 350°F.

Sift together the flour, baking powder, salt, cinnamon, and nutmeg.

Cream the margarine with the sugar until fluffy. Beat in the egg, lemon rind, and vanilla. Stir in the flour mixture, one-third at a time, adding alternately with the milk. Blend well to make a stiff dough. Spoon half of the dough into another bowl. Blend in a few drops of red food coloring to tint the remaining dough pink.

Pinch off a teaspoon of each color dough. Roll each into pencil-thin strips about 5 inches long. Place side by side. Press the ends together. Twist into a rope. Bend the top to form a cane. Place 1 inch apart on an ungreased cookie sheet. Bake for 10 minutes. Cool for 5 minutes before carefully removing from the sheet.

Store between layers of waxed paper in a tightly covered container. These can be made 2 weeks in advance.

The Search for An Authentic Hermit

The first time I made the cookies known as hermits, Edward said, "These are very good cookies, but they are not hermits."

It was, as the political commentators say, a matter of form — not substance. The hermits of my husband's childhood were two-inch by four-inch bars. Hermits, according to Betty Crocker and her Minneapolis test kitchens, were little round cookies.

Both recipes called for raisins and spices. But the New Hampshire version used molasses, making the bars a rich brown, while light brown sugar made the Minneapolis hermits a pale imitation.

My friend Rene Marchand grew up in Fall River, Massachusetts, where at least one bakery specialized in hermits. "They definitely were bar cookies, and they had a lot of raisins in them. I have bought a lot of hermits since, but none has ever tasted quite as good as those from the bakery," he said.

How, I wondered, did the cookies get their name? Were they invented by someone who preferred solitude to society? Were recipes for the cookies handed down through families? Was there an official recipe for hermits?

Posing those questions, I put an ad in the Personals section of the newspaper. My ad looked quite tame compared to those searching for "a vegetarian soul mate, nondrinker, nonsmoker, open-minded, for quiet times in remote farmhouse."

Nevertheless, the response was quite brisk.

One writer said hermits originated on Cape Cod in the town of Harwich. They were packed in the sea chests of the whaling and trading ships. The cookies stayed fresh for months because they contained dried fruit, molasses, nuts, and spices from the West Indies.

Originally, a hermit was more cake than cookie. As they evolved, the cookies became almost as chewy as fudgy brownies. In fact, some Yankees insist hermits are not only the ancestors of both blondies and brownies but that the formula is foolproof. "You can't spoil a hermit," wrote Eleanor Early in her 1954 *New England Cookbook*, adding, "if you don't have currants, use twice as many raisins."

It turns out that not every New Englander shapes the cookie batter into bars. Helen Tawse of Keene, New Hampshire, wrote that her mother, Angeline Cushing, "always dropped the dough from a spoon." Her mother, Mrs. Tawse said, is ninety-eight.

Jackie Clark, also of Keene, sent along a recipe hand-written in 1874 by her ancestor Sarah Loring of New Boston, New Hampshire. Not having access to a photocopier, Mrs. Loring used pen and ink to write her favorites in a four-inch by six-inch account book. Her version of hermits calls for butter, sugar, eggs, currants, cloves, one nutmeg, cassia, and saleratus. The former is a spicy oil related to cinnamon and the latter is baking soda. The cryptic instructions for Sarah's hermits said only, "Mix thick enough to roll."

Lois Leach of Westmoreland, New Hampshire, is also of the drop-cookie school of hermits. Mrs. Leach spent the World War II years in Westerly, Rhode Island. "Many of the local ladies took on the job of keeping the cookie jars full at the many small Coast Guard and Navy stations on the shore. Sugar was rationed, and we were given one cup of sugar for each batch made. The recipe I used made many cookies using the allowed one cup of sugar. It is a drop cookie and a simple one so I have used it ever since."

Mary Lautzenheiser, a professor of home economics at Keene State College, sent a Maine version of the recipe.

"The enclosed was given to me by a friend who considers it to be an authentic Maine recipe. The recipe was handed down at least as far back as her great-grandmother, who was a native of Maine. My friend says the dough properly is always shaped into long, log-like rolls which flatten and spread when baked — if the dough has been mixed to the proper consistency. The baked strips are then cut to form squares. The drop cookies are *not* authentic hermits."

Professor Lautzenheiser added that there is a hermit recipe in the 1896 edition of the *Fanny Farmer Cookbook*. However, Mrs. Farmer directed her readers to roll out the dough and cut it into rounds.

Ruth Palm, the librarian for the town of Swanzey, New Hampshire, sent a recipe that appeared in the *Boston Herald-Traveler* in the 1960s when it took the Easy Elegance prize. The recipe calls for spreading the dough in a jellyroll pan. When Mrs. Palm first tried the recipe in 1968, she made the marginal note, "Very good. Be sure not to *overbake.*"

A community cookbook published in 1932 by the Helping Hand Society of Wolfeboro, New Hampshire, describes its version of the hermit as "an old kind of old-fashioned cookie."

The chocolate chip cookie was once a plain old-fashioned New England cookie, too. Then it was discovered by Bloomingdale's and Neiman Marcus, and it became a gourmet $16-a-pound fast food for the rich.

May the authentic hermit live on in obscurity and may it never come in contact with a quarter of a cup of amaretto.

Hannah's Hermits
Yield: 4 to 5 dozen hermits

1 cup butter, softened
½ cup sugar
1 cup molasses
2 eggs
3½ cups unbleached all-purpose flour
½ teaspoon baking soda
1½ teaspoons ground cinnamon
½ teaspoon ground cloves
½ teaspoon ground ginger
½ teaspoon ground nutmeg
½ teaspoon ground mace
1 cup raisins
1 cup coarsely chopped walnuts
Water (optional)

Cream the butter with the sugar until fluffy. Beat in the molasses and eggs. This step can be done in a food processor.

Stir the flour, baking soda, and spices together until mixed. Add to creamed mixture. Stir in raisins and nuts. The batter will be stiff. If you think it is too stiff to spread, add a little water. Preheat the oven to 350°F.

Place 3 to 4 cups of the batter on a greased cookie sheet. Spread the batter until it is ½ inch thick. Bake for 10 minutes. Test the hermits by placing the tip of a knife into the center. If it comes out clean, the cookies are done. If not, bake for 3 minutes more. Do not overbake because these are chewy cookies.

When the cookies test done, remove them from the oven. Use a pancake turner to cut the cookies into 3 lengthwise strips. Then cut crosswise into 2-inch pieces. Using the pancake turner, remove the cookies from the sheet and place on a cooling rack.

Angeline Cushing's Hermits

Yield: 11 to 12 dozen cookies

1 cup butter, at room
 temperature
3 cups firmly packed
 brown sugar
¼ cup sour cream
4 eggs
6 cups pastry flour
2 teaspoons baking
 soda
1 teaspoon ground
 nutmeg
1 teaspoon ground
 cinnamon
2 cups raisins
2 cups currants
1 cup broken nut
 pieces
Grated orange rind
 (optional)

Preheat the oven to 350°F.

Cream the butter with the brown sugar until fluffy. Beat in the sour cream. Add the eggs, 1 at a time, and mix well.

Stir together the flour, baking soda, and spices. Add to the butter-egg mixture and stir until mixed. Fold in the fruits, nuts, and orange rind (if desired).

Drop by the tablespoon onto a greased baking sheet. Press down lightly with a fork or a spoon. Bake for 12 to 15 minutes, or until lightly browned. Remove the cookies from the cookie sheet and cool on a rack. The recipe can be cut in half, if desired.

Lois Leach's Easy Hermits

Yield: 50 cookies

¾ cup margarine
1 cup sugar
1 egg
⅓ cup molasses
2¼ cups unbleached
 all-purpose flour
2 teaspoons baking
 powder
1 teaspoon ground
 cinnamon
1 teaspoon ground
 cloves
½ cup raisins

Preheat the oven to 350°F.

Cream the margarine with the sugar until fluffy. Add the egg and molasses. Beat until thoroughly mixed.

Sift together the flour, baking powder, and spices. Stir into the egg mixture. Stir in the raisins. Drop the batter by the teaspoon onto a greased baking sheet. Bake for 12 to 15 minutes, or until lightly browned. Remove the cookies from the baking sheet and cool on a rack.

Here's to a Cup of Kindness

I wasn't aware there was a candied fruit shortage until I asked the man at the produce counter where he kept the fruit.

"We're all out," he said with a shrug. "No one expected people to buy a lot of things for baking this year."

This was the third store I had visited in search of candied cherries; but when you live upcountry, you expect to hunt for cinnamon sticks, pine nuts, and ladyfingers. In the big city, the problem is deciding which of three stores on the block has the pinkest peppercorns, the freshest goat cheese, or the flakiest chocolate croissants.

But I was in a country market holding my shopping list and a recipe for a spectacular dessert called Christmas Eve Cake.

We had been invited to a Christmas Eve dinner, and I had offered to bring dessert. Ordinarily, we cannot afford the calories in cakes and pastries. But every now and then, I enjoy taking the time to experiment and create a work of edible art.

The cake consisted of two layers of sponge cake brushed with brandy, and an almond and chocolate flavored frosting decorated with the cherries, chocolate stars, and whole toasted almonds.

Of course, the cherries could be omitted. I began looking around the store for a substitute. I met a friend in the baking supplies aisle, and I blurted out the news of the shortage.

She is a talented and artistic cook and understood my disappointment. She mentioned there was a good supply of candied fruit in a small store on the other side of town.

Well, the day was a stormy one, travelers' warnings had been issued, and the roads were already slippery. I knew I might regret spending the time on the candied cherry search — especially if driving home turned out to be hazardous or impossible.

Safe at home, I candied some cranberries and the results were acceptable but not as attractive as I would have liked. The candied berries were a too-deep red and some were rock hard while others were soft and sticky; biting was the only way to tell which was which.

The cranberry project reminded me of my attempts to candy the violets of spring to decorate the pastries of winter like a Bonwit Teller package. But I always lost patience and enthusiasm at the point where you are supposed to apply 260°F. sugar syrup with a tiny brush to the fragile blossoms.

In any case, I decided to go with the cranberries and assemble and decorate the cake after work the next day.

When I arrived at the office the following morning, there was a beribboned carton of candied cherries on my desk. Despite the shortage, the snow and ice, and her own hectic holiday schedule, my friend had come through.

Once again, I realized the very best gifts are the unexpected acts of kindness. "Never resist an impulse to do something kind" is the way my mother put it. Among her good impulses were homemade bread and the German fast-night cakes delivered warm to delighted neighbors.

My Christmas Eve Cake was well received. I was pleased I could give something of myself to people I love. And there were enough candied cherries left over to make two batches of favorite Christmas cookies for two good neighbors. Suddenly, I had found the time to bake those cookies. And the cookies themselves became the occasion for two spontaneous visits.

All of which reminds me of an aphorism I heard a long time ago, "The giver never knows where a gift ends."

Barbara Hall's Miniature Cheesecakes

Yield: 20 cheesecakes

1 pound (2 packages, 8 ounces each) cream cheese, softened
½ cup sugar
2 eggs
1 teaspoon vanilla extract
20 vanilla wafer cookies
1 can (8 ounces) fruit pie filling

These little cheesecakes are simple to make. They make a nice ending for a buffet dinner because they are also simple to eat. For a larger event, Ms. Hall suggests using several kinds of pie filling to make an attractive display. "Blueberry, pineapple, and cherry look so attractive on the dessert table," she advises.

* * *

Preheat the oven to 375°F.

Cream the cream cheese with the sugar. Add the eggs and vanilla.

Drop the vanilla wafers, flat side down, in the bottoms of twenty 2½-inch-wide foil baking cups. Place the cups on an ungreased baking sheet.

Fill each cup three-quarters full with the cheese mixture. Bake for 15 to 20 minutes until just golden. Watch closely and do not overbake. Do not be alarmed if the cheesecakes puff up, then fall or crack. The fruit filling covers all. Remove the cheesecakes from the oven and cool. Top with the pie filling and serve.

Tina's Christmas Cake
Yield: 10 to 12 servings

Cake

5 eggs, separated
1 cup sugar
Grated rind of ½
  lemon
1 tablespoon lemon
  juice
2 tablespoons cold
  water
¼ teaspoon cream of
  tartar
1 cup sifted
  unbleached all-
  purpose flour

Filling

½ cup rum, brandy, or
  Marsala
2 ounces semisweet
  chocolate, broken
  in pieces
1½ cups (12 ounces)
  ricotta cheese
6 tablespoons sugar
1 teaspoon almond
  extract

Frosting

1½ cups (12 ounces)
  ricotta cheese
6 tablespoons sugar
1 teaspoon almond
  extract

Decorations

3 ounces semisweet
  chocolate
12 whole almonds
12 candied cherries

Here is a very festive cake. It is not difficult to make, but it does take time. The cake is begun 24 hours before serving. The decorations may be prepared at that time to make final assembly easier. You will need a food processor and a small star-shaped cutter. I used the cutter from a set of long-neglected canapé cutters I had stored in my pantry.

* * *

Preheat the oven to 350°F. Grease and flour two 9-inch round cake pans. Have all the cake ingredients at room temperature.

Beat the egg yolks with ½ cup of the sugar until fluffy and lemon colored. Stir in the lemon rind, lemon juice, and water.

Beat the egg whites and cream of tartar until peaks form. Gradually add the remaining ½ cup sugar to the egg whites and continue beating until stiff, not dry, peaks form.

Gently stir the flour into the egg yolks, then gently stir the stiff egg whites into the yolk mixture. Blend the ingredients thoroughly but carefully.

Pour the batter into the pans. Bake for 30 minutes, or until the cake begins to shrink away from the sides of the pan, and the point of a knife inserted in the center of the cake comes out clean.

Place the cake on a rack and cool for 10 minutes. Then invert the pan and allow the cake to cool thoroughly before removing from the pan.

To make the filling, brush the top of each cake layer with the rum, brandy, or Marsala. Using a food processor, process the 2 ounces of semisweet chocolate until finely grated. Remove the chocolate to another bowl.

Process 1½ cups ricotta cheese, 6 tablespoons sugar, and 1 teaspoon almond extract until thoroughly blended and light. Add the chocolate and process just until blended. Spread 1 layer with the filling and top with the second

layer. Cover tightly with plastic wrap and refrigerate overnight.

To make the frosting, process the remaining 1½ cups ricotta cheese, 6 tablespoons sugar, and 1 teaspoon almond extract until thoroughly blended. Spread the frosting over the sides and top of the cake.

To make the star decorations, melt the remaining 3 ounces semisweet chocolate in a double boiler. Spread the chocolate thinly on a piece of waxed paper. Using a small star-shaped cutter dipped in hot water, cut out 12 stars.

Toast the almonds by placing them in a 300°F. oven for about 12 minutes, stirring once or twice.

To decorate, place a star, a cherry, and an almond at the edge of the cake and repeat the pattern to encircle the cake. Refrigerate the cake until serving.

Lily's Christmas Cookies
Yield: 4 dozen cookies

1 cup unsalted butter
⅔ cup sugar
2 eggs
2 teaspoons almond
  extract
2¼ cups unbleached
  all-purpose flour,
  sifted
24 candied cherries,
  cut in halves

Have all the ingredients at room temperature. Preheat the oven to 375°F.

Cream the butter and sugar together until light. Add the eggs and beat until the mixture is fluffy. Beat in the almond extract and gradually add the flour. Mix just until the flour is blended in.

Chill the dough for 20 minutes in the freezer or for 1 hour in the refrigerator.

Using a tablespoon of dough for each cookie, shape the dough into a ball and place on a lightly greased cookie sheet. Flatten the cookie and top with a cherry half.

Place the cookie sheet in the middle rack of the oven. Bake for 8 minutes, or just until edges turn a light golden brown. Remove the cookies from the baking sheet and cool on a rack.

Note: Lily's Cookies also add a festive note to February holidays, such as Valentine's Day and Washington's Birthday.

Florence Huntley's
Forgotten Cookies
Yield: 4 dozen cookies

3 egg whites
½ teaspoon cream of
    tartar
1 cup sugar
1 teaspoon vanilla
    extract
1 cup black walnuts,
    coarsely chopped

These meringue cookies bake while you sleep.

* * *

Preheat the oven to 400°F.

Beat the egg whites with the cream of tartar until soft peaks form. Beat in the sugar gradually, and beat until the whites hold a stiff peak.

Fold in the vanilla and nuts. Drop by the teaspoon onto an aluminum-foil-covered cookie sheet. Place in the preheated oven. Shut the oven door and turn off the heat. Do not peek. Leave the cookies in the oven overnight. Store in an airtight container.

Note: You can substitute ordinary walnuts for the black walnuts or replace the nuts with a package (6 ounces) of chocolate chips. A southern version of Forgotten Cookies calls for 1 cup chopped pecans and the chocolate chips.

A Festive Triple-Chocolate Dessert

When faced with January's long, cold nights, I contrive ways to prolong the cheerful holiday season. I keep the Christmas tree alive and decorated for as long as possible.

How, I wonder, can I relieve the sadness I feel when the last box of ornaments is packed away? Some years, I keep a string of tiny lights wound around an antique mirror to brighten the northern New England evenings.

In other parts of the world, the festive Yule season extends well beyond the New Year. In Vienna, for example, the season called *Fasching* begins with Twelfth-night and ends on Shrove Tuesday, the day before Lent begins.

Fasching is a season of wine and waltzing. Some popular people must juggle invitations to as many as five balls a week. Which brings to mind the Viennese cake, sacher torte, a dessert consisting of a chocolate sponge cake glazed with apricot jam and frosted with a bittersweet icing. Chocolate sprinkles — or jimmies as they are called in New England — make this a triple-chocolate treat.

The first time I tasted sacher torte, I was bitterly disappointed. The time was just after World War II, and I was a little girl. During the war, people made eggless, butterless, and less-less cakes. Gradually chocolate, eggs, and butter appeared again in the stores. My mother bought a large box of baking chocolate and told us she was going to make something very special called a sacher torte.

Mother had clipped the recipe from a local newspaper, where she had read that the torte had been invented by an imperial chef at the Sacher Hotel in Vienna.

We six children anticipated the dessert, it seemed, forever. When the cake was served at last, it was indeed a warming sight. But the first bite told another story. The sacher torte tasted terrible. Something was dreadfully wrong. All the precious ingredients had been wasted.

Days later, the newspaper was bombarded with letters from angry cooks who splurged on the chocolate, butter, and eggs after years of wartime deprivation. It turned out the sugar had been omitted from the list of ingredients. I now understand how it happened. As a newspaper food editor, I am surprised and relieved that such errors don't happen more frequently than they do.

Years later, when I visited Vienna, I tasted sacher torte at the Sacher Hotel. It was wonderful and worth the wait. In Vienna, it turns out, the precise formula for sacher torte is as controversial as the American recipes for chili con carne or clam chowder. But all Viennese bakers do agree there should be some sugar among the ingredients.

Like the New England lobster, maple syrup, and blueberry jam, sacher torte is shipped all over the world.

Here, then, is my favorite version of sacher torte. For best results, bring the ingredients to room temperature before you begin.

That means if you live in a drafty, old farmhouse as I do, you should stoke up the wood stove or turn up the furnace a few degrees before you begin. Otherwise, folding the beaten egg whites into the chocolate cake batter can be difficult, because the melted chocolate hardens quickly in the cold kitchen.

Sacher Torte

Yield: 6 to 8 servings

Cake

5 squares (1 ounce each) semisweet chocolate
½ cup butter, softened
¾ cup sugar
6 eggs, separated
¾ cup sifted unbleached all-purpose flour
½ cup ground blanched almonds

Glaze

½ cup apricot jam
8 squares (1 ounce each) semisweet chocolate
4 ounces chocolate sprinkles (optional)

Preheat the oven to 350°F. Lightly grease and flour the bottom and sides of a 9-inch springform cake pan.

Melt the 5 ounces chocolate over hot water. Cool slightly.

In a large bowl, cream the butter with ½ cup of the sugar until fluffy. Beat in the egg yolks, 1 at a time. Gradually beat in the melted chocolate and then the flour and almonds.

Beat the egg whites until frothy. Add the remaining ¼ cup sugar and beat until stiff. Fold the egg whites into the chocolate mixture. Pour the batter into the prepared pan and spread lightly. Bake for 50 minutes. Remove from the pan and cool on a wire rack for several hours.

Split the cake in half horizontally, using a sharp knife. Use the bottom of the cake for the top layer. Use about ⅓ of the jam to join layers. Spread the remaining jam thinly over the top and sides of the cake.

Melt the remaining 8 ounces of chocolate over hot water. Spread the chocolate smoothly over the cake. Make a border of jimmies by pressing them into the chocolate at the bottom edge of the cake.

Chocolate Truffles

Yield: 64 truffles

1 egg white
2 tablespoons cognac or Grand Marnier
2 tablespoons unsweetened cocoa
1½ cups sifted confectioners' sugar
1½ cups finely chopped almonds
1½ cups grated unsweetened chocolate
¾ cup sweetened condensed milk
1 tablespoon butter

Line an 8-inch square pan with aluminum foil.

Place the egg white, cognac or Grand Marnier, cocoa, confectioners' sugar, and almonds in a small bowl and stir to mix. Using your hands, knead together. Place in the foil-lined pan and pat into a layer covering the bottom.

Place the chocolate in the top of a double boiler. Melt the chocolate over hot — not boiling — water. Add the sweetened condensed milk and butter and cook for about 7 minutes, or until the mixture thickens. Pour this mixture over the nut layer in the pan. Spread evenly.

Let cool for at least 2 hours. Then cut into 1-inch squares. Store in an airtight container.

World-Class Peanut Butter Fudge

Yield: 3½ pounds

4 cups sugar
1 cup milk
1 tablespoon butter
1 cup peanut butter
1 cup Marshmallow Fluff
⅔ cup sifted unbleached all-purpose flour
1 teaspoon vanilla extract
½ cup coarsely chopped walnuts

It's difficult for me to imagine any layperson who knows more about eating for good health than my friend Marjorie Graves. At any moment, she's likely to reel off a list of potassium-rich foods, estimate the sodium count in a stalk of celery, or name the amino acid that promotes a good night's sleep. In her kitchen, she practices what she has learned and prepares fresh, unprocessed food that tastes wonderful.

However, every Christmas season, Marjorie relents, and to the joy of young reporters, she makes great batches of creamy peanut butter fudge. She brings her specialty to the newspaper office wrapped in cellophane and shiny red bows.

Flour may seem like a surprising ingredient in fudge, but Marjorie points out that it gives the fudge a nice texture.

* * *

Mix the sugar, milk, and butter in a heavy saucepan. Cook to the soft-ball stage (238°F.). Remove from the heat and add the peanut butter, Marshmallow Fluff, flour, vanilla, and walnuts. Mix well, but there is no need to beat. Pour into a greased 9-inch by 13-inch pan. Let set until hard. Cut into 1-inch squares. You should have about 117 pieces. Store in an airtight container at room temperature.

Index